PENGUIN BOOKS

Lev's Violin

'Prepare to be transported to Italy . . . Attlee's words paint
a picture of an Italian town as the sun's rays fade in the
rose of evening and the crowds mill in the piazza. It's a
seductive picture . . . a lovely story, written to haunt you,
just in the way that beautiful violin music does'
Nuala McCann, *Irish News*

'Elegant and ambitious . . . Attlee pursues her story with
honesty, diligence and open-mindedness . . . An original
and refreshingly unorthodox approach to history'
Jamie Mackay, *Guardian*

'Delightful . . . Attlee's love and unbounded
enthusiasm for Italy shine through the pages'
Graham Elliot, *Spectator*

'Charming . . . Attlee tells the story in easy,
luminous prose' Ivan Hewett, *Daily Telegraph*

'Reading *Lev's Violin* is like listening to a fine instrument:
thoroughly relaxing but also exciting, fun yet deeply
serious . . . with constant surprises and charms'
Tobias Jones, author of *The Dark Heart of Italy*

'Illuminating, engrossing . . . a wide-ranging exploration
of the history and cultural significance of the Italian violin'
Jonathan Buckley, *TLS*

'Charming and original . . . Attlee has the natural storyteller's gift'
Stephen Walsh, author of *Debussy*

'In limpid, searching prose, Helena Attlee shows us how music
can cast spells but also bridge the distance of centuries'
Marina Benjamin author of *The Middlepause*

'This book uses the history of one violin to explore what
objects mean to us, how they change us and what we invest in
them . . . charming and witty . . . Attlee writes with gentle humour,
her graceful style delivering some wonderful descriptions'
Helen Michetschlager, *The Strad*

ABOUT THE AUTHOR

Helena Attlee is the author of the award-winning *Sunday Times* bestseller *The Land Where Lemons Grow*. She has worked in Italy for much of her life, and it has been the inspiration for many of her books.

Lev's Violin

An Italian Adventure

HELENA ATTLEE

PENGUIN BOOKS

PENGUIN BOOKS

UK | USA | Canada | Ireland | Australia
India | New Zealand | South Africa

Penguin Books is part of the Penguin Random House group of companies
whose addresses can be found at global.penguinrandomhouse.com

First published by Particular Books 2021
Published in Penguin Books 2022

001

Printed and bound in Great Britain by Clays Ltd, Elcograf S.p.A.

The authorized representative in the EEA is Penguin Random House Ireland,
Morrison Chambers, 32 Nassau Street, Dublin D02 YH68

A CIP catalogue record for this book is available from the British Library

ISBN: 978-0-141-99107-8

www.greenpenguin.co.uk

MIX
Paper from
responsible sources
FSC® C018179

Penguin Random House is committed to a
sustainable future for our business, our readers
and our planet. This book is made from Forest
Stewardship Council® certified paper.

For Moishe's Bagel, whose music is
the beginning of this story.

Contents

Contents

Prelude

I still remember everything, the warm night, the rows of seats, all taken, and mine right at the front. Music filled the darkened room, overflowing through open windows on to the streets of a small Welsh town. It doesn't matter now what Klezmer tune it was that made us restless on our chairs, or pulled some people to their feet and had them dancing in those narrow spaces. What matters is the moment when two steps took the violin player to the front of the stage, and all the other instruments, accordion, piano, drums and double bass, fell silent. For that is when I heard the violin speak for the first time, with a voice powerful enough to open pores and unbuckle joints, and a shocking intimacy that left us all stupid with longing for emotions larger, wilder, sadder and more joyful than we had ever known. And after the applause faded and the lights came up, my old friend Rhoda turned her laughing face to me and said 'How dare he speak to us like that? We're married women!'

As we left the building I saw the violin player standing outside and so I went straight over to pass on Rhoda's joke, explaining she was an old friend in every sense, being well over eighty at that time. I suppose I expected him to laugh and move on, but instead he drew me aside and muttered something about what he called his violin's 'mongrel history', as if this could be an explanation, or perhaps even an excuse, for the seductive depth and unsettling power of its music. 'I've been told it was made in Italy at the beginning of the eighteenth century,' he said, 'but it came here from Russia. Everybody calls it Lev's violin, after the guy who owned it before me.' An Italian violin called Lev? It could hardly have been more unlikely.

Then he turned away, saying 'Have a look if you like,' and pointing at the case leaning against the wall beside me. When I opened it and looked inside, my immediate impression was of an object so weathered and streamlined that it looked like something you might find on the tideline of a beach, a bit of driftwood perhaps, a water-worn pebble or the sleek remains of some sea creature. Glancing at violins in the past, I had always perceived them as a mix of curves and corners, their crisp edges accentuated by a dark line of inlaid wood. But life had worn away the edges and knocked the corners off Lev's violin, so that in places its seams were almost flush with its sides, as if music lapping at its outline for centuries had eroded them like a fragile coastline.

Lying in its case, it looked as inanimate as some small piece of furniture, but then I bent down to pick it up. I had probably held more birds than stringed instruments at that time in my life, and the feeling reminded me of scooping a hen from its perch, its small body always so much lighter than I expect, and pulsing with life. Hens smell of hen, but Lev's violin had a strong, human scent, an intimate residue of sweat left by generations of musicians. Until then I had thought of violins as precision instruments, bright with varnish that caught the light and played with it, as if they were determined to be seen. But this violin was a very quiet matt brown, and it wore a history of mishaps on its body, a labourer's uniform of dark scars and deep scratches as expressive as the lines on an old face.

Looking down, I realized I was holding the violin like a newborn child, supporting the back of its head with one hand, and its body with the other. But it was no baby. Its life already spanned centuries, it had been worn to the bone by countless years of hard work, and had travelled the world alongside generations of musicians, living with them in close and urgent proximity. After years of hard service, its body was ingrained with the DNA of everyone who had ever played it, so it felt as if I was holding much more than an instrument in my hands. It must have absorbed the anxiety of its players along with the grease from their fingertips, responded to their different bows and bowing techniques, to the tone of their muscles and the tone of their voices. Over the centuries it had made infinitesimal shifts in its own structure to accommodate the peculiarities of every new player and the emotions and ideals of each new era, so that it had become a physical record of all those people's lives, of the journeys they made and the music they played.

I am not sure how long I had been standing there before the violin player reappeared, now with a pint in one hand and a roll-up in the other. 'It was actually made in Cremona,' he said, 'but when I took it to be valued I was told that it's absolutely worthless.' I have never been able to forget these words. In those days I knew so little about violins and the way they are valued that I would have been better placed to value a dog or a cake. Nevertheless, even I knew that the small Italian city of Cremona was home to Antonio Stradivari, and I also knew – as everyone does – that Stradivarius violins are some of the most valuable instruments in the world. To say your violin comes from Cremona is to award it the highest pedigree available to a stringed instrument, and I was outraged to think that Lev's violin, with its exalted provenance, long history and wonderful voice, could be deemed worthless. In fact, hearing 'Cremona' and 'worthless' in the same sentence was almost as unsettling as the vigorous and passionate voice I had heard coming from the violin's scarred old body.

If the fiddle player had told me his instrument came from anywhere else in the world, I might have remembered for a year or so the sensation of holding it, replayed the sound of its beautiful voice in my head for a while, and then forgotten all about it. But here's the thing, I have loved Italy ever since I was an adolescent, and I have worked there, in one way or another, for much of my adult life, either leading tours or doing the research for books and magazine articles. And yet despite years of travelling backwards and forwards, years spent looking over my shoulder at Italian history, I had never been to Cremona. I knew nothing about the violins that made it famous, and I was just as ignorant about the music they played.

Standing on the dark street that night, I was curious about these things for the first time.

Now the crowd began to thin as people called out their good-nights and walked away, but the violin player seemed in no hurry to leave. I kept him company for a little longer while he finished his cigarette. My mind raced with the thought of all the stories encrypted in the modest creature I still cradled in my hands, stories that promised to take me to entirely new places in the country I had known for so long, new destinations in the familiar landscape of Italian history, new territories to discover and explore. Eventually, I handed back the violin and we said goodnight. But as I walked off into the dark, I had a powerful sense of having left something fragile and very precious behind, and I had to fight an impulse to run back and look for it. And if I had run back, what would I have found? Only the empty pavement where we had stood, or perhaps the musician still standing beside the violin, which was certainly fragile and very precious to him, but nothing to do with me.

When I tell you I found myself thinking about the violin again and again over that summer, you will imagine I hadn't enough to think about, but actually it was a particularly busy time. Or you may suppose it wasn't the violin that distracted me, but the memory of its player, with his gorgeous face and passionate music, but that's not so. Our meeting had coincided with a sad, strange moment in my life, because my mother had just died and we were emptying the house of her possessions, uprooting objects that flourished there throughout my childhood and setting them adrift to search for new homes. Many of them had their own stories, stories I thought I knew because I had heard them again and again over the years. Now that both my parents were gone, I realized I had never listened, so that some of those tales were already lost for ever. This sadness made the stories I sensed hovering around Lev's violin seem even more intriguing and precious.

In the days and weeks that followed I found myself imagining the wide piazzas and narrow streets of Cremona, where winter fog would settle like a lid. I started to people the city by reading books about famous Cremonese violin-makers, and I was soon enthralled by the way they had transformed the violin from a gentle newborn into the powerful and technically brilliant instrument that has never been surpassed in four hundred years. And then I got lucky because someone offered me a few days' work in Milan, only a short train ride from Cremona. I jumped at the chance to go, already planning to steal time afterwards in the hometown of Lev's violin.

First Movement

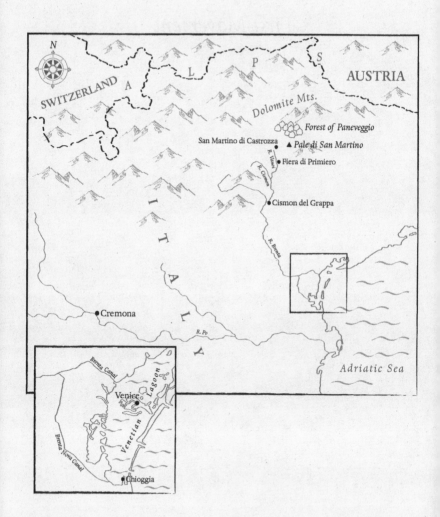

Child of Many Fathers

Cremona and the Modern Violin

I arrived as the sun went down, and customers in crowded bars were spilling out on to broad piazzas to sip Aperol spritz the colour of sunset. The violin makers' workshops in the narrow streets were closed, but there were plenty of instruments displayed in their windows, their rich, golden-brown varnish catching the sun's last rays. I was riding a bike grown old and lame from clattering over those cobbled streets. It belonged to my landlady in Cremona and it had a broken basket and a hooter that didn't hoot, a dry chain and slipping gears, but it carried me all over the city at a steady pace, its squeaky commentary unfolding with every turn of the pedals. It was rush hour and I had already been overtaken by a Franciscan friar pedalling at manic speed, and again by a woman with a small spaniel fast asleep in her bike basket. Anyone watching me as I stopped to look into the window of every violin maker's workshop I found could be forgiven for thinking I was in Cremona to buy a violin. But the only one I was seriously considering was made of chocolate, and I saw it in a *pasticceria* near the duomo. I had no need of a new instrument, but I longed to know more about an old one, and so I had come to Cremona to see where the life of Lev's violin began. I had read a few histories of violin-making by then, and older books generally named this as the place where violin-making had been reimagined, and the old-fashioned fiddles rasping out their music all over Europe had evolved into the sophisticated violins we know today. As I cycled round the little streets it dawned on me that Cremona was not only the beginning of the story of Lev's violin: being there put me at the heart of the story of every great Italian violin ever made.

There were luthiers' workshops, or *botteghe*, everywhere, but not all were at street level. When I saw one advertising its presence with a violin hanging from a first-floor balcony, I realized I must look beyond the shop fronts in obvious locations on main streets. I left my bike leaning on a pile of other bikes against a wall and began scrutinizing the brass plaques by big front doors to find the names of violin makers with workshops hidden inside *palazzi* lining the *corso*, or main street. Then I pressed my face to dusty windows concealing more workshops down small side streets. I even slipped through the back door of a bar and found a workshop cleverly hidden under a mountain of scrambling wisteria on the far side of a courtyard.

Luthiers lucky enough to work in premises at street level had lots of different ideas about the best way to use the space in their shop windows. Some dwelt on the golden era of violin-making in Cremona, turning their windows into early eighteenth-century drawing rooms, where violins balanced on gilded chairs were trapped in conversation with the plump cherubs lolling about on pedestals beside them. Other luthiers displayed their instruments alongside an apothecary's-worth of antique jars containing the arcane ingredients used for making violin varnish in Cremona ever since the sixteenth century, and some just filled all the available space with body parts, so that instead of a complete violin, cello or viola, you saw only the pale curve of an unvarnished belly, beautiful scrolls or a half-carved back displayed among tools and a drift of pale wood shavings. Each workshop was different, but every one was the view into a tradition stretching back to Andrea Amati and the first chapter in the story of modern lutherie in the mid-sixteenth century. Lutherie, or *liuteria*, is the craft of making stringed instruments of any kind, and whether in Italian or English the word preserves the memory of a time when most of those instruments were lutes in either language. I have always liked the Italian habit of transferring the titles of ancient skills like this to new ones. Needing a haircut in Italy means a visit to the *parruchiere*, who would once have cared for your *perucca*, or wig, and an unfortunate incident in the car is followed by a bill from the *carrozziere* for fixing your bodywork, rather than your *carrozza*, or carriage.

I got up early after a first night in Cremona and rode my borrowed bike back into the city centre along narrow roads lined by the peeling pink and ochre walls of palaces, and under jasmine that tumbled from first-floor balconies, inviting the whole street to ponder its thick scent. I have read that most weddings in Cremona are between people who have lived in the city all their lives, and on that morning I had no trouble understanding why they might never want to leave that beautiful place.*

Violins and their culture seemed to penetrate Cremona at every level. The Museo del Violino in Piazza Guglielmo Marconi is dedicated to their history, and there were shops selling the wedges of mountain maple and the Alpine spruce used for making them, stacked in cross-hatched piles. When I picked up a piece of maple it caught the morning light and showed off its silky tiger stripes. The pile of spruce revealed many different shades of gold because, as the keeper of one of those pungent places explained, when cut spruce is exposed to sunlight, 'it tans just like we do.' As well as shops selling violin-making materials, there were tool shops and shops stocking ingredients for varnish, shops full of books about violin history and violins emblazoned on tea towels, fridge magnets and keyrings. Customers in that *pasticceria* in Via Solferino could choose between white chocolate (unvarnished) or plain chocolate (varnished) violins. And as if violins were not getting enough attention already, I found myself cycling down streets named Andrea or Nicolò Amati, Guarneri del Gesù or Carlo Bergonzi after Cremona's greatest violin-makers, and across a piazza called Stradivari. The theme continued that night when I ate at Ceruti, a restaurant named after one of the last generation of eighteenth-century violin-makers in the city. I was the only customer for *marubini*, a circular pasta that is as old as Cremona's oldest violins, for it has been stuffed

* David Gilmour, *The Pursuit of Italy: A History of a Land, Its Regions and Their Peoples*, Allen Lane, 2011, p. 397.

with meat and served bobbing about in a bowl of broth ever since the sixteenth century. That night the Ceruti made its *marubini* with a surprising and delicious pumpkin and amaretti stuffing.

If you know anything about old instruments, you will think me stupid for not taking photographs of Lev's violin with me to Cremona. That will be because you already know that a violin wears the colour of its varnish and the details of its carving as a bird wears its plumage, and, like good ornithologists, luthiers in Cremona can identify most Cremonese instruments at a glance. However, it wasn't the identity of Lev's violin that interested me. I just wanted to get back to the roots of its story, and find out about the luthiers who had transformed both the violin and a small city on the banks of the River Po, turning Cremona into an international legend that still has the power to draw musicians and dealers from all over the world.

Cremona is often referred to as the 'birthplace' of the modern violin, but when I visited the violin museum I found its curators adopting a much more diplomatic tone. They were careful to describe the violin both as the product of Andrea Amati's genius and the logical conclusion to a slow process of evolution that had simultaneously unfolded in many places. For when Amati set to work in Cremona, there were already other craftsmen rethinking the violin down the road in Brescia, just as they were in the German town of Füssen, and in Poland and Bohemia.

If you could have analysed its DNA, you would have found traces of three different instruments in Amati's modern violin. The first was the *violetta*, or old-fashioned fiddle. It began as a crude contraption nailed together from planks, with five strings that lay flat over its fingerboard and could only be used to play chords. *Violette* had been played on the streets of Italy ever since the Middle Ages, and their robust voices and rhythmic chords were also heard keeping time at the kind of dances that happened in fields, barns and piazzas. The violin's other ancestors were the rebec, with its pear-shaped body, and the *lira da braccio*, which had two bass strings. Features from these three instruments had come together in plenty of violins, violas and cellos in Italy long before Amati came along. Should you ever get the chance to go to Saronno in Lombardy, you will find a likeness of the string family captured just before Amati got to work. They are the stars of a fresco in the cupola of the duomo painted by Gaudenzio Ferrari in 1535. His real subject was an angelic orchestra, but, unlike old-fashioned angels, who always played rebecs and lutes, his are modern thinkers, and they play a cello, a viola and a violin. Ferrari was a string player himself, so although he must have known the congregation gathered far below could never see the finer details, he painted the instruments with forensic precision. They are caught at the penultimate stage of their long evolution, showing off the narrow waists, overlapping edges and curved bellies and backs they inherited from the *lira da braccio*, and the lateral tuning pegs they adopted from the rebec. These instruments are already much more sophisticated than the *violetta*, for ever since the end of the fifteenth century, luthiers had been using glue instead of nails to fix them together, so they could move freely without cracking or coming apart at the seams. By 1530 luthiers were also carving out the wood for backs and bellies to give their violins thinner and more flexible bodies, and wedging a vertical stick inside, which made them stronger, and passed the strings' vibrations more effectively between front and back when the instrument was played. These innovations made the violin more responsive to the player, giving it a generous, singing tone that was quite different from the coarse, old-fashioned voices of its ancestors. And yet this was not the end of the journey, because Ferrari's portrait of string family members captured their likeness on the eve of transformation in Cremona.

Amati set up his workshop during the bleak days of Spanish rule in Cremona, a time of 'darkest night' in Lombardy, according to Stendhal, when the power of the Church was unassailable, and monks taught people 'that to learn to read, or for that matter to learn anything at all was a great waste of labour'.* Nevertheless, the city was always a magnet for artists, craftsmen and merchants, who

* Stendhal, *The Charterhouse of Parma*, trans. C. K. Moncrieff, Everyman's Library, 1992, p. 4.

all used the River Po and its tributaries as their trade routes. Its musical culture was nurtured by a love of the private concerts, or *accademie*, that were regularly performed in the palaces of rich families willing to pay composers and musicians good money for entertaining them. In other Italian cities you get so used to seeing statues of Garibaldi or King Vittorio Emanuele II that you scarcely bother to read the inscriptions on plaques beneath them, but not in Cremona. It was a breeding ground for talented musicians and composers, and its piazzas are guarded by figures from this pool of home-grown talent. Claudio Monteverdi's likeness crops up all over the city. Born there in 1567, he became the greatest composer of his generation. Andrea Amati was still making violins while Monteverdi was a child, and it can be no coincidence that he grew up to be both a violinist and one of the first composers in Europe to write music specifically for instruments that were the talk of the town throughout his childhood in Cremona.

The city centre must have looked much as it does today when Amati was alive. The lovely Romanesque duomo and baptistery had both been there since the twelfth century, and the octagonal bell tower – known even in Amati's day as the Torrazzo – was built in the thirteenth century. Most of the huge piazzas that I rattled across on my bicycle would already have been built by then, and so would the elegant Renaissance palaces lining the streets, the colours of their painted walls already marrying well with the weathered brick and pale marble of the older buildings. Although this backdrop to Andrea Amati's life is still intact, we are clutching at straws when it comes to a backstory for the shadowy figure of lutherie's great hero. Someone called Andrea, 'occupation: instrument maker', crops up in a city census of 1526, but who knows if that was actually Andrea Amati? Nobody, it seems. However, his full name is recorded in the local archives in 1539, when he rented a house in the city parish of San Faustino, and we do know that he lived and worked there for the rest of his life, and that his family held on to the house for the next two hundred years.

Nobody knows where Andrea Amati trained, but Cremona had

always been home to woodcarvers, joiners and cabinet-makers because of its position on the River Po, a well-established route for barges travelling south laden with Alpine timber. The most accomplished woodworkers in the city carved the intricate decorations for the interiors of churches and palaces. They were often commissioned by the same patrons to make viols, the instrument of choice for amateur musicians among the aristocracy. Some people suggest that Amati began his working life in this way, accumulating skills that would become the foundation for his new career as a luthier.*

There is neither a contemporary biography nor a portrait of Amati – for who would have bothered with the likeness of someone as lowly as a craftsman in sixteenth-century Italy? Only a painter making his own self-portrait. And who among Amati's contemporaries would have taken the trouble to record the biographical details of his life? Sixteenth-century luthiers had no one to champion them in the way Giorgio Vasari championed artists in his *Lives of the Most Eminent Painters, Sculptors and Architects* and yet all we need to know about Amati is written into his work. Take the Andrea Amati violin on display in the Ashmolean Museum in Oxford. It was one of a set commissioned in 1563 for Charles IX of France by his mother, Catherine de' Medici, and its label describes it as the oldest surviving violin in the world. The commission alone is enough to tell you that Amati was at the top of his trade in Europe at that time, and yet the date on the violin also tells us that his success was not easily won. He was already about fifty-eight years old when he made it, and it had taken years of quiet and diligent work at his bench to achieve the international recognition that resulted in this triumph.

I had prepared for my trip to Cremona by going to the Ashmolean and seeking out Amati's violin. Like so many of the violins there, it was once part of a collection of instruments donated to the museum by W. E. Hill and Sons, an unrivalled firm of violin-makers, restorers and dealers founded in 1880 in London

* William Henry Hill, Arthur F. Hill and Alfred Ebsworth Hill, *The Violin-Makers of the Guarneri Family (1626–1762)*, Dover Publications, 2016, p. 6.

by William Hill. By the time William's sons, Arthur and Alfred, inherited the firm, they were becoming increasingly anxious about the welfare of the beautiful old Italian instruments passing through their hands to be repaired or sold. This was the inspiration for their altruistic plan to donate a collection of rare instruments to the Ashmolean, where they could retire from active service and be properly cared for. Discussions with the museum began in 1936, and the first instruments were handed over in 1939.

Small, neat and quintessentially modern, Amati's violin lives in a gallery full of instruments we no longer recognize, built to play music we no longer hear. In this room full of ghosts it displays a level of craftsmanship and an understanding of acoustics that put it at the cutting edge of late-Renaissance technology. For sixteenth-century listeners accustomed to the gentle voices of viols, lutes and other old-fashioned stringed instruments, the relatively strident sound of modern violins could be deeply shocking. The English poet and playwright John Dryden captured the reverberations of this shock in his 'A Song for St Cecilia's Day', a poem written in 1687 to celebrate the power of music and honour its patron saint. He describes the sounds of various instruments, and while he seems to accept the trumpet's 'loud clangour' and the 'thundering' drum, there is something more ambiguous about his description of 'sharp violins' proclaiming:

> Their jealous pangs, and desperation,
> Fury, frantic indignation,
> Depth of pains, and height of passion,
> For the fair, disdainful dame.

Compare this to a description of the sound of viols written at about the same time by the lawyer and historian Roger North, and you begin to sense the contrast between their familiar, old-fashioned voices and the unsettling, modern sound that Dryden describes. Viols now sound like 'a sort of harmonious murmur', which North described as having more in common with 'a confused singing of birds in a grove' than with 'musick'.*

The modern body of Amati's violin glows with the biscuit-brown varnish that was his trademark. It wears the worn remains of King Charles's motto curling like a banner around its ribs, and some of the gold and black of a painted pattern clinging to its back. Fine-boned and elegant, it has a single line of 'purfling' that neatly encompasses its belly and is drawn to the delicate points known as bee stings in its corners. This word is almost unknown outside the world of lutherie, but should you find the occasion to use it, 'to purfle' is 'to decorate something with an ornamental border'. On a violin, purfling is the narrow strip of black-white-black inlay around the edge of the belly and back. As with so many features of Amati's design, the purfling was both practical and aesthetic. Busy, hard-working violins can easily be dropped or knocked, and purfling has always been there as a buffer, designed to prevent the fatal spread of a crack from the instrument's edge to its heart.

If you – like me – always lazily assumed that the sound of a violin came from its strings, think again, because of course the surface area of the strings on Amati's violin was much too small to shift the air around them and make sound waves. The haunting voice of his all-new instrument was produced when the tiny vibrations from the strings were amplified by its body, which was just a resonating chamber made from wood, a box full of air. The vibrations passed first through the bridge that Amati placed beneath the strings, and then into the violin's belly. By carefully carving out the wood for the belly he had made it so thin and flexible that it moved in time with even the smallest vibrations, amplifying them, and passing them on to the back of the instrument through a little wooden peg he called the *anima*, or 'soul'. Belly and back now vibrated together, and the bass bar, a length of tapered spruce fitted along one side of the belly, picked up lower-frequency vibrations, so that now the entire body of the instrument was vibrating and churning out sound through the f-holes in its belly.

* *Ibid.*, p. xxviii.

When Amati started work in Cremona, luthiers in other places were making violins in a variety of dimensions. He cut through this confusion and made it an established practice to produce violins of only two sizes. One was exactly the same size as the violin you will see if you ever go to the Ashmolean, and one was fractionally larger. The perfectly balanced outline of these instruments became the template for every luthier in three generations of his own family, and every other luthier practising in Cremona. What an extraordinary achievement – but that was not all. Andrea Amati also perfected a system for making violins that would be followed first by his own descendants and then by all the other luthiers who came to work in the city, so that even 150 years later Antonio Stradivari was employing exactly the same method as Andrea Amati had used to make his violins.

Amati built his instruments around an internal form or mould that he cut from a slab of wood. He began by gluing the instrument's sides – or 'ribs' – around the curvaceous perimeter of the mould. As soon as the glue dried he removed the mould, and then the ribs became a template for cutting out the new violin's belly and back. That's the nub of it, the thing that makes Cremona violinmaking different from other traditions. In France, for example, they use an external mould. This is a wooden template used to trace the shapes of a violin's back and belly on to the wood from which they will be cut. While this approach produces an identical result time after time, Amati's internal mould always creates a slightly different outcome, so that to this day every instrument made in Cremona is new minted, unique. Amati's classical form for the scroll, or 'head', of the violin was another extraordinary technical achievement. His design brought all the angles and curves of the form together, creating the illusion that it was completely round, and this became the blueprint for scrolls carved by luthiers all over Europe.

Amati's violin was perfectly designed to play late-Renaissance and baroque music, but by the mid eighteenth century its owner would have been struggling to reach the high notes and produce the volume demanded by the fashionable classical repertoire. If he could see his violin in the Ashmolean today, Amati might be shocked by all the changes made to enable it to play this new music, but without them his instrument would have become as redundant as the tool for some forgotten craft. Updating his violin involved removing the neck and replacing it with the longer one, set at a slightly steeper angle than the original. This made the instrument easier to play in the high positions demanded by classical composers, and increased the volume and projection of the violin's voice by putting greater pressure on the strings. As time passed, these modifications were made to any violin worth hanging on to – and yet here's an interesting thing about stringed instruments. It doesn't seem to matter how many parts of the violin, viola or cello have been replaced, and it doesn't even seem to matter if the shapes of their bodies have been re-tailored in some way. Just as the garden spade whose handle I have had to replace again and again will always be my mother-in-law's spade, an Amati will always be an Amati, however many adjustments and alterations it endures.

Andrea Amati died in 1577, passing the business on to his sons, Antonio and Girolamo. Antonio had entered the workshop about twenty years before his father's death, but Girolamo was around two decades younger than his brother, so that by the time he joined the business, Andrea was nearly seventy and Antonio was an experienced luthier of thirty-five. Antonio trained his younger brother, and after their father's death they continued to work together, labelling their instruments 'Brothers Amati'. After little more than a decade, however, Antonio broke free from the family firm and went off to set up an independent *bottega*, or workshop, nearby. Girolamo had no sons, and he might have thought of taking on apprentices at this point. However, there was already a strong tradition among the Amati of making business a strictly family affair, and so instead of looking elsewhere, he recruited two of his sons-in-law, Vincenzo Tili and Domenico Moneghini, to assist him at the workshop in San Faustino.

The Amati family continued to dominate lutherie in Cremona for well over a century, making violins into the stars of the musical world and laying down the principles of a craft that is still synonymous with the city. I had known nothing about them or the history of stringed instruments when I heard Lev's violin for the first time, but now I had become a bicycling biographer to the violin family. I had studied every detail of its ancestry and visited its birthplace, where I found Amati's 450-year-old system for making violins still being taught to lutherie students, and still being used in workshops in the shady streets and glittering *palazzi* all over town.

Musical People

How Violins Became Stars of the Musical World

Cremona was teaching me the musical facts of life: how violins were conceived and made. But what about the world they inhabited beyond the city walls? And how did they spend their days? This is what fascinated me now. I imagined violins emerging from the Amati workshop into a very musical world, because of all the tired old clichés about Italy one of the most persistent has it inhabited by people always on the verge of bursting into song. Like every other cliché, this one has some truth in it, for I remember being amazed by the sheer amount of music to be heard in Italy when I moved there for the first time. Of course it came as no surprise that gondoliers in Venice sang, but I hadn't expected to find singing taxi drivers in Rome, fruit sellers behaving like opera singers in Naples, or music drifting like smoke over the narrow backstreets of Florence during Il Maggio Musicale festival. Siena was my home in those days, and every time I piled into a car with friends and set off on a long journey, they would start to sing. Growing up in England, I had learned from an early age to keep my mouth shut whenever singing happened. Extraordinarily – to me – some of my Italian friends had voices no better than mine, and yet they sang with gusto all the way to the mountains or the sea. It took a while for self-consciousness to release its iron grip on my throat, but soon enough I was singing along to 'Le Sette colline di Roma', 'Bella ciao' and anything by Lucio Dalla – Italy's own Bob Dylan.

All this made a profound impression on me, but it was a very dilute experience compared with Italy in the second half of the sixteenth century, when Amati's violins emerged into a world so musical that it was almost guaranteed to appreciate them and explore the potential of their brand-new voices. In those days the Italian peninsula was divided into a series of enormous kingdoms ruled by foreigners, and tiny dukedoms, principalities and petty states that belonged to a few families, all jostling for power. This uneasy political situation meant that Italy was often torn apart by war, and yet, despite the bloodshed, plagues and famines that were war's closest relations, Italian society was saturated in music from top to bottom. Out on the streets it was everywhere. Beggars swapped it for coins on corners, and travelling musicians scraped a living by summarizing the news headlines, setting them to music and performing them for a fee. Tradesmen, craftsmen and bands of mercenary soldiers all sang songs as distinctive as the tools of their trades or the uniforms they wore. These drinking songs, working songs and rousing patriotic songs added another layer of sound to the din in city taverns and the clamour of church bells on the streets, while beyond the city walls music echoed through the fields, barns and forests of the Italian countryside, where peasant farmers used local tunes and songs to ease the drudgery of their days, liven up their celebrations and mark every important occasion in the agricultural year.

Behind the massive doors of city palaces it was easy for violins to access a society in which men still modelled themselves on the perfect gentleman, immortalized by Baldassare Castiglione in his bestseller, *Il Cortegiano* (*The Courtier*), published in 1528. Among his many skills this ideal man could play several kinds of musical instrument, and violins soon formed natural alliances with rich and fashionable young men striving to be ever more accomplished. You started your training young in those families, and so violins also found their way into the hands of children obliged to take music lessons as part of their education. In some places – such as sixteenth-century Venice – people even seemed to value music above other forms of literacy, for while less than a third of wealthy merchant families in the city owned a book, it's said that virtually all kept at least two musical instruments in the house.* One of them would often have been a viol, long the instrument of choice among the upper classes. As the sixteenth century progressed, however, these large, flat-topped instruments gave up their privileged position to the fashionable, modern violin.

Amati violins continued to be the best in the world for well over a hundred years after they were first produced by Andrea in Cremona, and like diplomats they moved between the illustrious courts of Italy's different rulers. Their music was a vital ingredient in the triumphalist, allegorical pageants and processions that ruling families used to celebrate their power and nurture *magnificenza*. This cult of magnificence was the dazzling blaze around the court of every ruling family in Italy, helping it to square up to its enemies, impress and intimidate its subjects, and convince everyone of its God-given right to rule. A banquet put on by the Este family in 1529 was a particularly beautiful example of the role of music in the chemistry of *magnificenza*. There is a vivid account of this musical feast in a book by Cristoforo Messisbugo called *Libro nuovo nel quale s'insegna a far d'ogni sorte di vivanda* (*New Book in Which the Preparation of Every Kind of Food is Taught*), published in 1549. As steward in the household of Cardinal Ippolito d'Este, Messisbugo was in charge of organizing the spectacular feast that the cardinal gave to celebrate his brother's marriage to Princess Renée, daughter of Louis XII of France. The table music performed during the meal was the responsibility of Francesco della Viola, the aptly named court musician, a role for which he was paid as handsomely as the cardinal's own valet. The party took place in 1529, a little too early for the modern violin. Consequently Messisbugo's account serves as a wonderful insight into the arcane family of stringed instruments that existed alongside violins before Andrea Amati's breakthrough in Cremona.

The banqueting table was set out in the gardens of Ippolito's

* Patricia Fortini Brown, *Private Lives in Renaissance Venice*, Yale University Press, 2004, p. 123.

palace in Ferrara, among trees festooned with flowers. Sixteen musicians gathered under a canopy decorated with greenery, and, as darkness fell, servants lit torches among the trees and candles on a table spread with a white cloth and laden with glittering silver, cut glass, vases of flowers and gilded sugar sculptures. There were eighteen courses to get through, each made up of several dishes and accompanied by music chosen to reflect the flavours and scents of each course, and by singing, juggling and performances by acrobats, dwarves and dancers. Deafening music for three trombones and three cornets accompanied a mighty sturgeon decorated with the family coat of arms and served up as a first course with garlic sauce, while pike's entrails fried with oranges, cinnamon and sugar, and strewn with tiny blue borage flowers, seemed to call for the gentler sound of a flute and oboe. French pastries, artichokes, fermented apples and oyster pies were a job for a viol, three bagpipes and three flutes, while fried squid, crayfish in a French sauce and macaroni *alla Napoletana* were accompanied by singers dressed as peasants pretending to cut the grass. The guests, who must surely have been exhausted by sensory overload, were offered bowls of perfumed water to wash their hands before the eighteenth course was served. Then they picked at toppling piles of pistachios, pine nuts and melon seeds, bowls of candied orange and lemon rind, ice cream and nougat, while listening to the plucked strings of a cittern, a tiny kit fiddle of the kind used by dancing masters while demonstrating steps to their pupils, and six viols.

Andrea Amati's violins emerged into the world thirty years after this magnificently musical feast. At first they were like powerful racing cars with novices at the wheel, for neither the musicians who played them nor the composers who wrote their music had the skills or understanding to exploit their true potential. Initially they played music written for *ogni sorte di strumento*. When a composer wrote these words at the top of a new piece, it meant you could perform it on any instruments you chose. Within forty years of Amati's first violins emerging from Cremona, however, composers had begun to write music specifically for them. The first to properly explore the violin's technical possibilities was Monteverdi with *La Favola di Orfeo*, an entertainment cooked up in 1607 for Duke Vincenzo Gonzaga and his friends in Mantua. It combined music with drama, poetry, dancing, painted scenery and beautiful costumes in a recipe known simply as a 'work' – or *opera* in Italian. In the third act, Orpheus attempts to persuade Charon to ferry him across the River Styx by singing 'Possente spirto'. The violin accompaniment to this haunting aria became a benchmark for brilliance among early seventeenth-century violinists. And yet, within a few years the skill of such players evolved so much that the challenges Monteverdi set for them would come to seem almost childish. He explored the violin's powers of expression again during the sword fight in *Il Combattimento di Tancredi e Clorinda* in 1624. Here he used *pizzicato* – or plucked strings – to imitate the clashing of Tancredi's and Clorinda's swords as they fought doggedly to kill, and *tremolo* – a rapid and repeated note – to mimic their agitated breathing. These techniques intensify the drama of that tragic scene, and ratchet up its emotional impact in a way that is as effective today as it ever was.

If the violin had drawn a campaign map for its rapid domination of musical culture in Italy, all the activity would be in the north. While Amati's violins made their resolute invasion from Cremona, other violins from northern cities such as Brescia, Mantua, Ferrara and Venice swelled their ranks. Then came a plethora of new music written especially for them. Venice would feature large on their campaign map now, because it was the most prolific printer and publisher of music in Europe. Other cities – Rome, Milan, Naples, Florence and Ferrara – had their own printers and publishers in the sixteenth century, but Venice was the only place with companies dedicated to the printing of music, and consequently it produced more sheet music between 1530 and 1560 than the whole of the rest of Europe put together.*

* Elizabeth M. Poore, 'Ruling the Market: How Venice Dominated the Early Printing World', *Musical Offerings*, vol. 6, no. 1, Article 3, 2015, pp. 49–60. https:// bit.ly/2kpKmCk

The unique conditions that enabled music publishing to thrive in Venice were a gift to the violin. Other cities did not have the money to sink into that new and highly specialized business at the end of the fifteenth century, but Venice did. Its wealthy merchants were always looking for new investments, safe in the knowledge that the Republic had put a legal framework in place to ensure fair rewards for anyone willing to tie their money up in high-risk enterprises.*
Their investments funded the specialist equipment and the high wages demanded by artisans with the skills to design and manufacture the necessary fonts, and then meet the challenge of aligning the notes correctly on the stave during the slow and expensive process of double-impression printing. At first this was the only way to print music, and it meant printing the same page two or even three times. The stave was the first thing to be printed, and then the paper was run through the press a second time so that the notes could be carefully overlaid on to it, and a third time for the words. When Amati set to work, however, printers in Venice had long since adopted the single-impression printing technique invented in London. New music could now be printed faster, less expensively and in greater quantities, which all combined to enable printers and publishers to increase their profits and penetrate new markets. New music written for violins rolled off the presses, full of virtuosic flourishes that only they could perform. When it came to its dissemination, Venice was yet again uniquely well placed. The city had been distributing goods it imported from Asia all over Europe ever since the Middle Ages, and now violin music travelled through the same distribution networks, so that the craze for violins and their music in Italy spread like a lovely infection to the rest of Europe.

Before Amati worked his magic, violin players and their instruments had very rarely been seen at court or in wealthy households. Nobody liked the voice of either the player or the instrument in those refined circles, where one was considered too working class and the other too loud and coarse. As the sixteenth century drew to

* *Ibid.*

an end, however, everything changed, for by now the social status of both violins and their players had been transformed, and they were welcome at every level of Italian society. By this time the Amati name was famous for lutherie all over Europe, and Cremona's monopoly of the trade was well established.

By now my notes about the life story of the violin in Italy, and of Lev's violin in particular, had begun to fill the tattered pages of the notebooks I carried with me everywhere in Cremona. And I may as well admit that I was even beginning to nurse a fantasy about being able to prove the real worth of Lev's violin.

Pilgrim in Cremona

The Great Violin-making Dynasties

Every evening the streets of Cremona would fill with students cycling through the city in droves. Draping themselves effortlessly over the crossbars of each other's bikes, laughing and chatting, they flew through the side streets like flocks of low-flying birds. One evening they swept me along with them. I can think of no other city where cyclists, walkers and drivers get on so well, for there was never a cross word as we glided on and off pavements and down pedestrianized streets, despite our absolute illiteracy when it came to road signs. I would have stayed with the flock for longer, but our destinations were different. They were on their way to a party, while I was just a pilgrim on a bicycle, devoted to visiting Cremona's holy sites of violin-making, and finding out all I could about the long ancestry of Lev's violin. Or that is what I should have been doing, but I was too hungry, so I peeled off from the cavalcade and dived through the door of a small restaurant in search of something to eat. I saw my mistake as soon as the door shut behind me, for I had stepped into a deep, dark club. '*Bonsoir*,' said the man behind the bar, and even more surprisingly, 'welcome to Brazilian music night'. I wandered out into the club's sunny courtyard where a struggling fig tree had been hung with wire sculptures, which were unravelling. Sitting down, I watched swifts working the sky, while musicians with a frame drum and guitars began to gather at their own table.

Sitting there with only a glass of wine for company, it struck me that both the club and the people in it were rebelling that night against the great classical traditions of Cremona's music and violins. This made me think about Nicolò Amati, whose grandfather Andrea had kicked off violin-making in the city, establishing a tradition that was faithfully upheld by Nicolò's father Girolamo and his uncle Antonio. Born in 1596, Nicolò was another rebel because he was the first member of the family to reconsider his grandfather's blueprint for the violin's design, creating a larger instrument that would be known as his 'Grand Pattern' violin. He also revolutionized the inward-looking culture of the family *bottega* in ways that would have a profound impact on the future history of violin-making in Europe. And as if those two achievements were not enough, Nicolò became one of the first and most influential teachers in the history of lutherie.

Nicolò was about twelve years old when he was apprenticed to his father Girolamo in the workshop attached to the Amati family's old house in the city parish of San Faustino. Girolamo had bought his much older brother Antonio out of the business in 1588, and since then he had been working with his two sons-in-law, Vincenzo Tili and Domenico Moneghini. Now Nicolò joined them, and at nineteen he was already working with his father to produce instruments that they continued to sign with the 'Brothers Amati' label, even though Antonio died in 1607. As his confidence grew, Nicolò began to play with the classical Amati design and dimensions, experimenting with the angle of the arching on the belly and back, and with the shape of the corners. He also selected maple for the backs of his instruments that had a more pronounced pattern, or 'flame', than the modest wood traditionally chosen by his relatives. By 1620, Nicolò was a fully fledged craftsman, and he had begun to take the lead in the Amati *bottega*.

The prestige of the family workshop is captured in a letter from the German composer Heinrich Schütz to the Elector of Saxony. Writing in 1628, Schütz advised his employer to order two Amati violins and three violas as soon as possible. Why? 'Because when such makers are gone,' he warned, 'violins of that quality will be unavailable.'* His words read like a presentiment, for the

---

* David Schoenbaum, *The Violin: A Social History of the World's Most Versatile Instrument*, Norton, 2013, p. 26.

inhabitants of Cremona were about to be caught in a perfect storm. Between 1628 and 1629 the city was gripped by famine. Then plague came to Lombardy, brought by French troops fighting in the Thirty Years War. When it spread like a biological weapon among Venetian troops on the battlefield, they fled, carrying the disease with them and taking it all over northern and central Italy. It killed 280,000 people in Lombardy alone, and Brescia, the other great centre for violin-making in the region, was the first place to suffer a full-blown outbreak. The death from plague of master luthier Giovanni Paolo Maggini in Brescia in about 1630 killed the lutherie tradition in that city stone dead, leaving Cremona with a monopoly of the trade until the mid-eighteenth century. Soon enough, however, it was Cremona's turn to suffer. 'This year, 1630, God our Lord has sent the plague all over Lombardy,' wrote the local priest. '. . . at Cremona it made its appearance in the early days of January, began to spread at the commencement of April, and raged to such an extent during the months of June, July, and August that the town was deserted and had the appearance of a wilderness.'*

The plague's impact on the Amati family and their workshop was catastrophic, for although Nicolò survived, over the course of a few days at the end of October and the beginning of November 1630, his father Girolamo, his mother Laura, two of his sisters and his brother-in-law and business partner Vincenzo Tili all died in quick succession. Plague had also decimated the musical world beyond the city walls, killing musicians and composers and creating a cultural vacuum that would take a decade or more to fill.

Almost alone in the workshop now, Nicolò received few orders in the years immediately following the plague. By the 1640s, however, business began to pick up again, and soon there was a renewed and ever-growing demand for Amati instruments from courts and wealthy clients from other regions of the Italian peninsula and abroad. The family had always kept the hard-won secrets of their trade to

* *Ibid.*, p. 7.

themselves, making the *bottega* a kind of closed shop by only employing family members. Now Nicolò must have realized he could only save the business by taking on apprentices from outside the family. No one knows exactly how many assistants he employed over the years, but so many people were recorded as living in the Amati house that it must have been a considerable number. Nicolò's role as a teacher was almost as important as his own output, for the names of young men listed in the census returns for the house in San Faustino read like lutherie's roll of honour. Among them are Giacomo Gennaro and Andrea Guarneri, who went on to become successful luthiers in their own right, and Bartolomeo Cristofori, who began his career as a luthier but was later credited with inventing the piano. Many others have been linked to the workshop because of their style, or their use of the term *Alumnus Nicolaus Amatus* on the labels they signed and then stuck to the inside of the backs of their instruments. Giovanni Battista Rogeri and Francesco Ruggieri are among them, and some say Antonio Stradivari trained there as well, because the oldest of his violins still in existence was signed with an *Alumnus Amatus* label. There were also several German names among the apprentices in the Amati household, and Jacob Stainer, star of the seventeenth-century Austro-German school of violin-making, is often named as one of Nicolò's pupils. There are no records to substantiate this suggestion, but nevertheless Stainer's early work bore such a strong resemblance to Amati's that he can be credited with bringing the tenets of Cremona violin-making to Austria, his home country, and to Germany and England where his instruments also sold.

Despite this new labour force, Nicolò could not begin to keep up with the demand for new instruments, and so his apprentices were able to go out into the world and create thriving businesses of their own. In this way techniques honed to perfection by the Amati and closely guarded by the family for over a hundred years spread throughout the violin-making world, so that there were soon luthiers in every major town and city in Europe working to Cremonese designs.*

* Roger Hargrave, 'The Cremonese Key to Expertise'. https://bit.ly/3oSZvfi

After encountering Lev's violin for the first time I had begun visiting the instrument collections you sometimes find in museums. At first the violins in their glass cases all looked the same to me, but as time passed I learned to study the details of each new instrument I saw. What shape were the f-holes in its belly, and where were they placed? What style was the scroll, and how finely was it carved? How were the corners shaped and what was the pattern of the purfling around their edges? What colour was the violin's varnish, and how deep was the arching – or vaulting – on its belly and back? Gradually I learned that these details distinguish one violin from another as clearly as features on a human face. Nevertheless, I found some of those instrument galleries sad places, where looking at the violins gave me much the same feeling as seeing caged animals at the zoo. Everything is wrong about seeing a violin behind glass. Violins are handled, closely, intimately, continually, while they are being made and throughout their careers, and they seem to yearn for human contact as keenly as wild animals yearn for freedom. I sensed this as I held Lev's violin for the first time, when it seemed to fit my hand and welcome even the touch of a stranger. This feeling reminded me – unexpectedly – of the sensation I used to have when I held the Neanderthal hand axe my father turned up while ploughing a field in Kent. He was always uncovering flint arrowheads and blades, but that great big ochre-coloured flint was by far the most glamorous and exciting discovery he ever made. He offered it to a museum but happily they let him take it home, where it lived on a windowsill within easy reach of our small hands. Superficially the two items could not have been more different. Lev's violin was as light as air, and the tension of the strings bore down on its body in a way that made it feel alive to the touch, while the flint axe was a dead weight, heavy and cold in the hand. And yet I can still remember the exact feeling of placing the heel of my small hand in the hollowed scoop made for that purpose and smoothed by use, and just as when I held Lev's violin for the first time, I had a sense of all the people who had held the axe before me. Sometimes I imagined as a child that holding it was like holding hands with the Neanderthal who had dropped it so carelessly in our field.

Next to Andrea Amati's beautiful violin in Oxford's Ashmolean Museum is an instrument made by his grandson Nicolò Amati in 1649. Violins are like those divorcees who hang on to the surnames of their famous ex-husbands long after the decrees nisi are signed, and the *Alard* takes its name from a relationship with Jean-Delphin Alard in the mid-nineteenth century. You can hardly blame it, because, as well as being a famous violin player and professor at the Paris Conservatoire, Alard was the son-in-law of Jean-Baptiste Vuillaume, one of the most famous luthiers, violin dealers and connoisseurs in Europe at the time.

Tucked away in its glass case, the *Alard* is a wonderfully curvaceous instrument, the sort you could fall in love with for its looks alone. Its back is made from mountain maple with a rippling flame deep enough to corrugate the surface of the wood. Its corners are extraordinarily long and narrow, which gives the whole instrument a fragile appearance, and there is not even a hint of an angle in the perfect undulations of the f-holes in its belly. Unusually for such an old violin, it still has its original neck, although this has been lengthened. The instrument is the colour of maple syrup, and I know that if it came out of its case the varnish would seem to dance in the light, changing its tone with every movement. Although it is in exceptionally good condition, a slight patina of marks on its body signals that it once lived life to the full. Some say the sound of a violin is closer to the human voice than that of any other instrument, and I remember looking at the *Alard*, mute behind glass, and feeling sure it had something left to say.

As I sat in the courtyard that evening, still waiting for the Brazilian music night to kick off in the club, I watched the barman emerge with a stein of beer on a tray. What happened next was unexpected, and for some reason it brought me back to thoughts of Nicolò Amati. The barman stopped beside the diminutive woman at the table next to mine, put down the beer on one yellow napkin and dabbed the back of her neck with another. Then he pressed the napkin to his lips and said to no one in particular 'this is what gives me energy', before ducking back into the dark doorway of the bar. Perhaps it was the flamboyancy of this small performance that reminded me of the man who quietly turned his back on a sacred family tradition and made the new instrument known as his Grand Pattern violin. The clients for this new design were virtuosi who wanted violins with voices strong enough to be heard by audiences in large spaces, or against the sound of a full orchestra – or ripieno – during a concerto grosso. There was something flamboyant about Nicolò's new model as well, because it was a little longer and quite a bit wider than anything that had emerged from the family workshop before, and in making it he had hit on proportions that are considered ideal to this day. In order to create the depth and strength of tone his clients demanded, Nicolò also made subtle changes to the shape of the arching to increase the vibrating area of the violin's body.

Nicolò remained a bachelor until he was almost fifty, but then made up for lost time by marrying and having nine children. His son Girolamo Amati II took over the *bottega* when his father died in 1684. He was a skilled enough craftsman, but violin-making was no longer the closed shop it had been when Nicolò began work, and Girolamo faced stiff competition from a new generation of master luthiers who were all trained by his own father. Beset by financial problems, he fled Cremona for Piacenza in 1697, where he more or less abandoned lutherie. His death in 1740 spelled the end of Cremona's first great violin-making dynasty.

One of Nicolò's earliest and most important apprentices was Andrea Guarneri, who worked alongside his master for a decade or so, learning to make instruments and living as a member of the family. He was so close to Nicolò that he even acted as a witness at his wedding, and continued to live in the house after his own marriage. Guarneri may not have been as fine a craftsman as Nicolò, but nevertheless his instruments were so well made that they have sometimes been mistaken for his master's work. He went on to found the next dynasty of luthiers to shape the history of violin-making in Cremona.

When they left the Amati household, Andrea Guarneri and his wife moved back to her old home at 5 Piazza San Domenico. Like the Amati before them, the Guarneri would remain in the same house and workshop for a hundred years. San Domenico was at the heart of the district known as Isola. Other luthiers soon joined Guarneri, so that it became a violin-making quarter where luthiers lived alongside cabinet-makers, carpenters, carvers and violin-case makers, as well as hinge-makers and shops selling the oils and resins for violin varnish. Andrea's son Giuseppe turned out to be the genius of the family. By 1730 everybody knew him by the nickname Guarneri del Gesù, on account of the little insignia printed after the name on his labels. It was a neat cross surmounting the letters IHS, the first three letters of the Greek word for Jesus. These days his violins are almost as valuable as Stradivari's, but this was not always the case. In a career lasting only just over twenty years Guarneri del Gesù had a few rich clients, but he generally worked for local farmers, shepherds and street musicians who could not afford expensive instruments. He found ingenious ways of economizing on materials for these customers. Of course he always selected high-quality wood for the bellies of his instruments, because this had the greatest influence on their sound, but he found that he could save money on the maple for their backs by using wood without the flaming generally beloved by other luthiers. He was never bound by the same rules of precision and craftsmanship that distinguished other makers in Cremona, and his instruments could be quite rough at times. Led by instinct, however, Guarneri del Gesù produced violins with such beautiful voices that many musicians still prefer their sound to that of a Stradivarius.

Guarneri del Gesù would never have considered himself a competitor to Stradivari – the old man who had already lived at 2 Piazza San Domenico for twenty years by the time he was born. Guarneri's violins were not especially sought after in his lifetime, but at the beginning of the nineteenth century a Guarneri del Gesù found its way into the hands of the Italian virtuoso Nicolò Paganini – and that was the beginning of a new chapter for Guarneri, albeit a posthumous one. It is said that Paganini was given the violin as a present in the early 1800s by the owner of a theatre in Livorno where he was due to perform.* He took to it immediately, calling it *Il Cannone*, The Cannon, and travelling all over Europe with it to give concerts. Their performances together provoked a mix of awe and terror among other musicians. Too jealous to admit he was simply the best violin player the world had ever heard, many put his prowess down to the violin, and consequently demand for del Gesù's instruments grew so fast during the 1830s that it soon began to rival the demand for Stradivarius violins.

You can't visit either Stradivari's or Guarneri's old houses today, because they were demolished in the 1930s. However, you can go, as I had done earlier that day, to the house at the far end of Corso Garibaldi where Stradivari began his career, moving in as soon as he was married in 1667. These days the ground floor of his old house is a kitchenware shop owned by a couple who were obviously all too used to visits from pilgrims like me. Could I look round? Yes I could, but as they were about to close they urged me to walk briskly through the long, narrow space with its displays of brightly coloured toasters, coffee-makers and novelty bottle openers, an experience that left me with nothing to report. Things were a little better upstairs, where I found one of the covered terraces that practical house builders in Cremona designed for drying laundry. Antonio and Francesca had six children, and while they all lived here Stradivari worked on gradually refining his craft. This was the slow beginning of a career that would eventually make him the colossus of violin-making in Cremona and the world, so that nearly three hundred years after his death his name is still famous.

I had just sat down on the terrace when the owner of the shop came upstairs to tell me they were locking up. He approached me with the caution you might display when interrupting someone's prayers, but he needn't have bothered. I was just wondering if

* Toby Faber, *Stradivarius: Five Violins, One Cello and a Genius,* Macmillan, 2004, p. 119.

Francesca had left space between the nappies on the washing line for Antonio to hang up his newly varnished violins to dry.

The Stradivari moved out of their old house on the *corso* in 1680. Their new home at 2 Piazza San Domenico was in the heart of the violin-making district, a stone's throw from the Guarneri at number 5, and not far from the Amati in San Faustino. A line drawing of the house can be seen in the book about Stradivari's life and work by the renowned London violin dealer and restorer W. Henry Hill and his sons, Alfred and Arthur.* Made in the 1870s, the drawing shows an elegant three-storey building with a shop front and a first-floor balcony. The shop on the ground floor was occupied by a tailor when the drawing was made, and probably still had a kitchen and parlour behind it, just as it did in Stradivari's day. Upstairs there were enough bedrooms to accommodate the eleven children Stradivari eventually had with Francesca and his second wife, Antonia Zambelli. Perhaps it was the sheer number of children in the house that made him favour the *seccadour* as a summer workshop. You could describe this typically Cremonese feature as a covered roof terrace or an open-sided attic. Either way, it could be reached only by a stepladder from the third floor, which would have cut Stradivari off from much of the day-to-day drama of domestic life with young children.

Stravidari made many of his violins in this rickety space, and perhaps the small and exquisitely decorated Stradivarius I saw in the Ashmolean Museum in Oxford was among them. Dated 1683, it was commissioned just after his move to Piazza San Domenico by the d'Este, one of the most important families in Italy. An inlaid pattern of delicate leaves and curling tendrils covers its scroll and ribs, the purfling is marked with a bold pattern of ivory circles and diamonds, and there is a shimmering mother-of-pearl star on the button. Dressed for a perpetual party, it was the work of a consummate craftsman who was about to emerge from the shadow of Nicolò Amati, and steal the show in Cremona.

---

* W. Henry Hill, Arthur F. Hill and Alfred E. Hill, *Stradivari, His Life and Work (1644–1737)*, Dover, 1963, p. 13.

Stradivari's move was swiftly followed by the death of his only real rivals. Jacob Stainer, another of the apprentices in the Amati household, who had become the most important luthier of the Austro-German school, died in 1683, followed by his one-time master, Nicolò Amati, in 1684. These two great losses to the world of lutherie marked the beginning of a season of success for Stradivari that would last fifty years. By now he had reached the acme of his powers. He was cutting f-holes, inserting purfling and carving heads with perfect skill, and producing instruments so accurately made and beautifully finished that they have never really been surpassed. His violins were designed to satisfy the virtuosi tackling new concerti composed by Arcangelo Corelli, Tomaso Albinoni and Giuseppe Torelli at the end of the seventeenth century that were bolder and more challenging than anything that had gone before. This was Stradivari's market, and he experimented with different moulds and adjusted the details of the design until he could produce violins powerful enough to speak clearly against the sound of a full concerto orchestra. In about 1690 he began to produce his own Grand Pattern violins, but he was forever experimenting with new models, and in 1700 he returned to the shorter, slimmer design that musicians found easier to handle. It was not until 1704 that he hit on a model with a tone and an acoustic that would satisfy him until the end of his long life.

Stradivari worked alongside two sons from his first marriage, Francesco, who was in the workshop with him, and Omobono, who spent most of his time dealing with commissions and sales. Stradivari did not pass on the longevity gene, and both his sons were dead within six years of their father. Francesco left the contents of the workshop to his half-brother, Paolo, Stradivari's youngest son by his second marriage. The bequest included nearly one hundred instruments, some of them incomplete, and all unplayed. In 1746 Paolo called on the luthier Carlo Bergonzi to bring the remaining stock into saleable condition. Bergonzi promptly moved into 2 Piazza San Domenico with his wife and children, and with assistance from his son, Michelangelo, he set about carving missing scrolls, fitting tailpieces, sound posts and pegs.

Antonio Stradivari's death in 1737 spelled the end of the golden age of violin-making in Cremona, but by now luthiers were producing violins in towns and cities all over Italy. Despite the higher number of luthiers in Venice, they could scarcely keep up with the demand for instruments from churches, opera houses, amateurs and private patrons, not to mention the *ospedali*, or charitable hospitals.

As darkness fell outside the bar, the musicians gathered at a table near to mine still showed no signs of launching into Brazilian music night. I thought they were poring over a sheet of music, but when I realized it was the cocktail menu, I decided to leave. Cycling home, I found myself quite grateful to Lev's violin. Don't suppose I ever imagined it was made by Stradivari or any of Cremona's other great luthiers, but I did think it might have been the work of an apprentice in some lesser workshop. And if not for it, I wouldn't have been cycling through dark streets, enjoying the first stars on a summer night in Cremona, or exploring the legacy handed down from father to son in the dusty workshops of the city's great violin-making dynasties. And yet despite this smug sense of satisfaction, I already knew I had not got back to the true beginning of the Cremona violin's story. It was seeing those piles of neatly sawn maple and spruce for sale that did it. They made me realize that one day I would have to travel far beyond the comfort of Cremona's pretty streets, and find my way to the remote mountain forests where the prime ingredient of Cremona violins grew.

Message from the Mountains

The Ancient Trade in Violin Wood

Ever since Andrea Amati started making violins, luthiers in Cremona have used Alpine spruce (*Picea abies*) from the Dolomites to create the bellies of their instruments. Over the centuries, so much of it has come from a forest called Paneveggio that the local tourist board likes to call it the *foresta dei violini*. I was already planning to spend a couple of weeks walking in the mountains that summer, and so my meandering journey now extended effortlessly to the trees growing on the upper slopes of the Primiero and Fiemme valleys, where the frayed edge of Italy leaches into Austria and Italian gives way to German long before the official frontier.

When I set out from Venice, the air streaming in through the car windows carried a summer's worth of heat and harvest smells, but, as the road began to climb, the temperature outside fell. By dusk I was between mountains on a narrow, twisting corridor of a road. A storm trapped in the valley below sent thunder ricocheting off the rocks, and torrents of rain sluicing across the road. Soon the lightning was so persistent that I fell into a paranoid routine of checking my mirrors, as if a police car might be pursuing me for some forgotten crime.

A final climb took me from the valley floor to Passo Valles, a pass linking the Travignolo and Biois valleys. Storm-addled and exhausted, I sprinted from the car to the door of a large refuge called Capanna Passo Valles. An ancient Saint Bernard with matted hair and a strident snore lay across the entrance. He didn't move an inch as I opened the door, so that I had to step across the bulk of his sleeping body. Inside, the *signora* behind the bar was pouring grappa for a few stragglers on their way to bed. She wore the traditional

Alpine costume of embroidered shirt, waistcoat and long skirt with a nonchalance that told me she would be wearing them again tomorrow, and the day after that. In bed, I listened to the storm crying itself to sleep outside, and thought about Amelia Edwards, that adventurous international traveller and author, whose book about visiting the Dolomites in 1873 was in my suitcase. During a summer spent exploring the mountains by mule, she observed a regular weather pattern of sunshine in the morning and early afternoon, followed by a gathering storm that would break in the evening and rage all night. On one occasion she complained of being kept awake as much by thunder and lightning as the continuous tolling of church bells. By five the next morning everyone in the village had formed a procession and begun to implore the Virgin to protect them from storms. The weather dried up nicely, but Edwards realized they were preparing for another procession at midday, this time to plead protection from drought. 'The good people of Caprile are difficult to please in matters of weather,' she wrote, and as I listened to the wind rattling the shutters and battering the thick walls of the refuge, I wasn't at all surprised. It struck me that, despite their beautiful voices, generations of Cremona violins have emerged from the discordant chaos of Alpine storms exactly like this.*

The real climbers, with their lycra-covered legs and crash helmets, were sleeping in the dormitory opposite my room. I heard them leave the next day at dawn, with a steady tramp of boots. This skewed the demographic of the dining room, so that most of my companions for breakfast were either very old or very young – not that this stopped them from polishing off the yoghurt and stewed fruit before I could get to them. Outside, Paneveggio nudged up to the edge of summer pasture, where the perfectly parallel trunks of Alpine spruce stood as straight as pencil strokes from a sure hand. Cremona violins are still born of the deep, damp, resin-scented

* Amelia Edwards, *Untrodden Peaks and Unfrequented Valleys: A Midsummer Ramble in the Dolomites*, Virago, 1986, pp. 169–71.

shade behind that palisade of trees, where moss makes no distinction between rocks, trunks and forest floor, covering everything with the same shining deep-pile carpet. Violins are made from several different kinds of wood, but it is Alpine spruce trees like those that have the most profound impact on their sound. Their wood is light, flexible and very strong, and this has always made it exceptionally good at transmitting the tiny vibrations from a violin's strings through its body, and for these qualities the wood is known as *legno di risonanza*, or resonance wood.

Amelia Edwards marvelled at the size of the 'primeval pines . . . rising from eighty to a hundred feet, enormous in girth, and garlanded with hoary grey-green moss, the growth of centuries'. Little had changed, although in those days the trees grew in the Habsburg Empire, which had owned the territory ever since the middle of the fourteenth century. Timber of any kind was of enormous value in pre-industrial Europe, when it was needed in vast quantities for building houses, barns and boats, making tools, producing charcoal to fire forges, kilns and furnaces, as firewood for cooking and heating, and wood ash for making soap and glass. When Andrea Amati was working to perfect his model for the violin in sixteenth-century Cremona, timber was as valuable as oil has been to us in the twentieth and twenty-first centuries. No wonder officials in the Habsburg Empire were busy devising a system that would make the production of resonance wood and all the other timber in the imperial forests sustainable. They protected the overall condition of the forest by only allowing approved *boschieri*, or woodcutters, to work there. Then they set a limit on the number of timber merchants extracting wood, insisting that each of them purchase a felling licence in Innsbruck. This management system became ever more sophisticated, and by the mid-nineteenth century Paneveggio was divided into squares like a giant chessboard, and the species, height and girth of the trees in each of these squares, or *particelli*, were meticulously recorded. The inventory of each *particelle* was updated every decade, and these records were the basis for all decisions about which trees to fell each year. This was the first scheme for forest management in Europe, and it is still in use at Paneveggio, and in many other places that once belonged to the Empire. It was so effective that Paneveggio supplies resonance wood to violin-makers across the world to this day. The forest is still managed in much the same way, although aerial photographs generally take the place of a tree-by-tree audit.

The first chapter in the life of any old Cremona violin was written by *boschieri*. They were local men, men who knew the height and girth of every tree on their patch, wore injury like a badge of office, and were tough enough and hungry enough to work that dangerous territory, never mind the risk of landslides, avalanches or flash floods. Despite this valuable skill set, *boschieri* were often too poor to own tools and so they depended on the timber merchants who employed them for the axes, bark scrapers, shovels and mattocks they would need to carry out their work during the season. Some men even took part of their pay in salami, bread, ricotta and wine, and looked to the merchants for shoes and the lengths of the coarse cloth needed for making clothes. You might call those *boschieri* lumberjacks if you were in Canada, but that's an odd name for men who also farmed the mountain slopes and had almost as many words for different qualities of grass as the Inuit are said to have for snow. *Boschieri* could tell the difference between 'grass for making milk' and 'grass for making meat', they recognized 'poor grass like the hair of a donkey' and knew where to find 'grass for calves as smooth as chocolate for children', and even 'grass to make goats drunk'.* Timber merchants were obliged to rely on these multitasking men for the first stage of the long process that would deliver every kind of timber, including resonance wood, to their customers, and yet the only really reliable thing about them seems to have been a stubborn determination to prioritize work on their own farms over working for timber merchants in the forest.

The first road to Primiero and its valley was not built until 1873. Describing the place before the road, Amelia Edwards said it had been 'as inaccessible for wheeled vehicles as Venice', because 'every avenue to the outside world was barred by a circle of passes, all of

* www.italy-tours-in-nature.com/vanoi.html

which were practicable for mules, but not one practicable through-out even for *carettini*.'* However, like so many other high-altitude communities in the Dolomites, the locals defied their isolation by using rivers as their means of transport and their trade routes. Ever since the Middle Ages, wood from mountain forests had been sent down the rivers Vanoi, Cismon and Brenta to Venice and other low-land cities, so that although the story of Cremona violins begins in a forest, it goes on to be all about rivers, clear, and so cold that dip-ping in a toe on even the hottest of August days banishes all thoughts of a swim.

There were many stages in the arduous process that eventually delivered resonance wood from the mountains to luthiers in Crem-ona, and the first was felling the Alpine spruce that grew on steep and awkward slopes. This demanded brute strength and great skill. Extracting felled timber could be equally difficult, and sometimes up to eight pairs of oxen and twenty *boschieri* were needed to extract a single tree from a difficult site.† Felling began as soon as the last snow thawed in early June. The *boschieri* left felled timber where it lay, only stripping the bark to allow the sap-soaked wood to dry out and make the timber lighter and easier to move. After making this prompt and enthusiastic start, they generally stopped work in the forest almost as soon as they had begun, because now the cows needed taking up the mountain to summer pastures. When they returned, the men would make good progress again until it was time for the first cut of hay in July, and then they wouldn't get back to the forest until it had been brought under cover. There was another break on St Bartholomew's Day, 24 August, which was

---

* Amelia Edwards, *Untrodden Peaks and Unfrequented Valleys: A Midsummer Ramble in the Dolomites*, Virago, 1986, pp. 226–7.

† Unless otherwise attributed, the information that follows about the wood trade between the Alps to Venice comes from Gianfranco Bettega and Ugo Pistoia, *Un Fiume di legno, fluitazione del legname dal Trentino a Venezia*, with maps and illustrations by Roswitha Asche, Quaderni di cultura alpina / Priuli & Verlucca editori, 2010.

celebrated in the local town of Canal San Bovo. The *boschieri* treated this as an official holiday, and timber merchants took this opportunity to gather their far-flung team together and settle their wages. The men often blew all their money on a drinking binge, so that brawls and knife fights were a regular part of the entertainment in Canal San Bovo during the *sagra*, or festival, which locals used to refer to as 'our own Wild West'.

There was a second crop of hay to cut before the men could return to the forest in September, and of course they downed tools again when it was time to fetch the cows off the mountain and bring them safely back to lower ground before the winter cold set in. Now they were ready to extract timber from the forest, and they got to work as soon as the first snow fell, tying ropes or chains around the trunks of felled trees on awkward slopes and skidding them across the snowy ground. Timber in more accessible places was loaded on to sledges pulled by oxen or horses.

By whatever means they managed it, the *boschieri* were contractually obliged to have all the wood neatly stacked at the forest's edge by St Martin's Day on 11 November. This marked the end of their responsibilities, for now the timber was in the hands of the *conduttori* . How would you translate this word, which has as much to do with driving the logs as leading them down the mountain like a guide? Whatever word you choose, it needs to describe men practical enough to invent solutions to every barrier they encountered while getting thousands of tons of timber down tricky mountain terrain to the river valleys. They depended on ice and snow to help them, and this obliged the *conduttori* to work outdoors day and night in the savage depths of winter. Over the centuries they invented several different strategies and structures for moving timber. In some places they could use snow-covered tracks to send the logs slaloming down towards the valley. If logs moved too slowly, the *conduttori* would pour water down the track and let it freeze overnight; if logs moved too fast, the men could scatter earth over the snow to slow them down. In places where there was no ready-made track, they had to construct log slides, or *risine*, from lengths of timber and anchor them firmly to the ground. These structures were dismantled at the end of each season, so that the wood they were made from could be sold along with the rest of the timber.

Merchants and *conduttori* spoke a mix of German, Venetian dialect and Ladino, a fusion between Latin and the Germanic languages spoken before the arrival of the ancient Romans. Walking in the mountains, I have often heard Ladino spoken by the locals. Crystal-clear communication was essential when logs were hurtling downhill, and so the men also developed an international working language over the centuries, for use at critical points on the slopes between Paneveggio and the river valley. It consisted of a specialized vocabulary of cries, warnings, whistles and gestures that could be used to communicate over long distances, or when it was too noisy to hear ordinary speech.

It was tough, dangerous work on the mountainside, and all kinds of accidents happened when timber was moving downhill at breakneck speed. Logs careering down a *risina* would jostle for space, and sometimes one or two would suddenly bounce or be pushed out, setting off on their own course and flattening anyone or anything in their path. The men at the top of the *risina* would yell a warning before they began to send the logs down, but there is a grim story from the end of the eighteenth century about a boy who decided to bunk off work and go up the mountain to watch a wedding procession. The foreman refused permission for this outing, insisting it was too dangerous to walk up the mountain while there were logs on the move. But we all think we are invincible when young, and so he set off uphill, along the edge of the log chute. After less than fifteen minutes, the shout 'Zoi! Zoi! Zoi' came down the mountain, a word in the specialized language of the *condotta* meaning 'Stop!' that was passed from man to man. A few minutes later a messenger ran down to say that a few logs had bounced out of the chute and smashed the boy to smithereens. Something about his disobedience must have angered the foreman, because instead of stopping work for a full day, the usual sign of respect after a fatality, he just sent four men 'with a sheet to gather the scattered remains' before sending word up the mountain to start the log flow again.

When autumn turned to winter on the mountainside, cold created perfect conditions for the *condotta*, and then the *conduttori* worked night and day for weeks on end, stopping only to eat meagre portions of polenta cooked up in camp kitchens, and seasoned with a scraping of salty cheese. Walking along that porous high-altitude border myself, I had to choose between eating very Italian polenta each night or the very Austrian *knödel*, or *canederli* as those bread dumplings are known in Italy, a choice that sometimes felt like a declaration of national loyalty. The *conduttori* had no such luck. Polenta was the fuel that powered them, and it was served in the same monotonous form every six hours.

All the timber had to be safely stacked in holding yards next to the river before the thaw. Wood from the Primiero would generally be sent down the rivers Vanoi, Cismon and Brenta when they were swollen by snowmelt and spring rain so that the log drive, or *menada*, could begin. Timber merchants prepared for the *menada* by hammering their personal insignias into the end of every tree trunk, so that, when the trunks were thrown into the water, they could be sure that their timber would not be claimed by anyone else. Only a tiny proportion of it would end up being used as resonance wood in Cremona, and yet from the sixteenth century it played its part in sustaining this important and complex trade.

The rivers carrying timber downstream towards Venice crossed the frontier dividing the Habsburg Empire from the Venetian Republic. They transported much more than timber, however, because this was also the boundary between northern Europe and the Mediterranean. As well as being trade routes for all the goods from the mountains and the valleys, those rivers were conduits for an exchange of languages and ideas between two cultures, of new styles of art, music, songs, stories, recipes, machinery and other inventions.

The timber was handed over to *menadàs*, or log drivers, on the riverbank, another specialist team who made their precarious living by driving timber downstream. Tree trunks made recalcitrant charges, suggestible to every current or whirlpool, prone to sulking in inlets, resting in shallows or joining forces with all the other logs and careering into the narrows to demonstrate exactly what 'log jam' really means. When that happened the *menadàs* were obliged to climb in among them, balancing on one bobbing, rolling log while prodding and pulling at the others with an *angér*, a tool neatly combining a spiked end with a log-sized hook. Timing was all, for as soon as the logs began to move again, the *menadàs* tried to jump clear, but accidents were as common here as they were in the forest or on the mountainside, and men were often crushed between fast-moving logs or swept downstream by the powerful flow of the river. Melting snow made the rivers rough and dangerously cold, and sometimes the men couldn't risk getting into the water at all. Then they had to rope themselves to a rock or tree, and try to release the jam while hanging suspended in mid-air. No wonder there are so many images of San Nicolò da Bari in the churches of small towns on the riverbanks – for he is patron saint of all those in danger on water.

Wood prized for its qualities in violin-making accounted for only about 1 per cent of the timber battling its way from the mountains to the sea. Sometimes the river was too shallow for it to float, and then the *menadàs* would send the timber on its way by calling in another group of experts to build dams. These river men would build with logs – what else? – and plug the gaps between them with mud and moss. If the shallows were too long for such a solution, the spruce trunks were sent down a permanent canal alongside the river. And where rapids interrupted the flow, they would be diverted down a custom-built slide.

Whether it was destined for building, burning or violin-making, timber attracted high taxes in the Habsburg Empire and as it crossed the frontier its journey was interrupted at a customs post in the form of a wooden barrage across the river. Here officials from the imperial offices in Salzburg checked every single tree trunk for owners' marks and made a note of the tax due from each merchant.

Soon the mountains were a distant memory and the rivers flowed gently through towns and villages. At Cismon del Grappa, the Cismon joined the Brenta Canal, whose banks were lined with sawmills, silk mills, flour mills, tanneries and small, furnace-driven industries of every kind, often linked to the river by their own small canals. The owners of all these businesses would buy the timber they needed for the year as it passed through town during the spring log drive. Logs could not be allowed to rampage downstream through these more densely inhabited areas, and for this reason there were raft-makers' workshops on the waterfront of every town. Here the logs were strapped together with hazel wands to make rough rafts, or *zattere*. Now the *menadàs* changed their job titles to *zattieri*, or raftsmen, with enough muscle to guide their awkward craft downriver. They stopped only to boil water and make the polenta that was still their staple diet. River men ate their polenta runny from a bowl, unlike the *boschieri* and *conduttori*, who preferred to handle it in solid slices. Rafts were both a system for transporting the timber and a means of transport in their own right, because the *zattieri* would carry passengers alongside mixed cargoes of firewood, chickens, cheeses, carved wooden spoons and other Alpine products for sale. There were harbours especially built for rafts in each town, and once moored, the *zattieri* could sell their goods, and eventually they would even sell the timber from which their rafts were made.

Chioggia, at the far end of the Brenta Canal, was the main marketplace for all the goods brought downriver. Timber was either sold there or taken to Venice through the Brenta Novissima Canal. There the spruce trunks were unloaded on the Fondamenta delle Zattere, built in 1519 expressly for receiving goods delivered to the city by raft. In the timber market, where the trunks lay motionless at last, each one was scrutinized by *lignaroli* – timber merchants – looking for wood to make the timber frames, joists, windows and doors of new buildings. The city's timber merchants also supplied the Venetian Republic's vast arsenal with mast timber, which happened to have many of the same qualities as resonance wood. Both needed to be light, flexible and free from the knots, pockets of resin or other faults that might weaken a mast – or distort the vibrations passing through a violin. These common properties were a lucky coincidence for Cremona's luthiers, because, when it came to getting the materials needed to build and maintain its fleets, the Arsenale had the power of the Venetian state and centuries of legislation behind it. It employed timber merchants on five-year contracts, stipulating both the quantity and quality of the timber they would supply.* They were punished with heavy fines for failing in either respect, so that luthiers in Cremona could always be sure of a steady supply of high-quality Alpine spruce into Venice. Instead of coming to Venice themselves, those luthiers generally depended on *lignaroli* to find resonance wood for them in the market, saw it into manageable lengths, and load it on to a barge for its journey to Cremona via Chioggia.

The *lignaroli* crossed the Lagoon back to Chioggia, making their way from there through canal and estuary to the mouth of the River Po, where they could unharness the oxen that had dragged the barge there, and raise a sail if conditions were right. Some cities on the riverbanks would allow them to pass without charge, but others levied a toll that could be set against the cost of dredging the river to keep the navigation channels open, maintaining the embankments and the towpath, and looking after the locks and sluice gates. Muddy jobs like these were the Po's gift to the local economy of Cremona and other places on its banks.

The journey upriver to Cremona was generally uneventful, unless snowmelt had transformed the peaceful river into a torrent. Then it became fierce and unpredictable, bursting its banks, altering its course, and forcing those merchant sailors to navigate a new and dangerous geography of sandbanks and muddy debris. The *lignaroli* also carried weapons on board – not because they could prevent accidents, but if the worst happened at least they could defend themselves against local gangs who roamed the riverbanks, ready to claim the cargo of any wrecked or beached vessel as their own.

* Karl Appuhn, *A Forest On the Sea: Environmental Expertise in Renaissance Venice*, Johns Hopkins University Press, 2009, p. 164.

The Po carried a steady traffic of *burchielli*, *berlingher*, *roscone*, *scaule* and *cesilie*, names from the watery dialect of Venice's boatyards and canals, and the dark taverns where the city's ship-wrights, fishermen and river merchants drank together. Ever since the ninth century these boats and flat-bottomed barges had been supplying all the towns and cities on the banks of the Po with neces-sities such as salt, wine, oil and dried fish. They also carried luxury goods brought back by galleys returning from long sea voyages: pepper and other exotic spices, silks, damasks, gold, silver, glass, medicinal plants and rare bulbs. Venice's exotic connections had their own importance for Cremona's luthiers, for although the bellies of violins in Cremona have always been made from Alpine spruce, their backs are made from maple (*Acer pseudoplatanus*). At first luthiers used local trees for this purpose, but when supplies ran low in the seventeenth century, they began to use mountain maple from the Balkans, because by cutting it across the grain they could reveal beautiful patterns in the wood known as 'curl' or 'flame'. They also needed ebony to make fingerboards and tailpieces and rosewood for making tuning pegs. These were both exotic, Indian woods, but this posed no problem, because Venice had trade links with India that went back to the Middle Ages.

The Po was also the conduit for outgoing trade, and, when they returned downstream, those boats and barges carried linen, wax, cheese, honey, leather and other products from inland villages and towns like Cremona to sell in Venice. And as well as transporting these physical cargoes, river merchants took news in both direc-tions, so that in the mid-sixteenth century the reputation of the first violins to be made in Cremona, with their beautifully crafted bodies and exciting modern voices, would soon have sped downstream to Venice and upstream to the Alps and northern Europe.

When I imagined the arrival of a timber barge in Cremona, I saw a lurching procession of handcarts and horse carts filling the cobbled streets linking Isola to the cargo dock on the Po, as luthiers and other craftsmen rushed to inspect a delivery of fresh timber. As soon as the hatches on the barge were opened, the sharp scent of freshly sawn wood and resin would fill the air, like a message from the mountains.

Every stage of the journey bringing resonance wood to Cremona had been a brutal struggle fraught with many different kinds of danger. By the time the timber arrived, it might already have done its job as part of a log slide or river raft, so that its cell memory was already forming around these harsh duties and its long soaking in the swollen waters of multiple rivers. Considering the suffering of the *boschieri*, the high-risk strategies of the *menadàs*, and the long, slow hours of work by luthiers in Cremona, I was startled all over again by the idea that anyone could describe Lev's violin as worthless.

Second Movement

Church Music

A Chapter in the Life of Lev's Violin

When I first heard the story of Lev's violin, it was as brief as a work of flash fiction. By now I had learned something about the making of it and the world into which it was born, and I was hungry to know more about the instrument itself. That didn't happen until the following summer, when I bumped into its owner again. We were both at a tiny music festival on the Welsh Borders, and it was another of those summer nights, made beautiful this time by a sliver of moon riding high above flags, rough grass and tents. It was not difficult to spot him in the crowd because of his hair. Dark, curly, shoulder length, it frames his face and makes him look like a figure in an Italian fresco – a ridiculous thought, because he soon told me he was born in County Durham.

It was quite a complex story to tell in the dark, with the music getting louder and dancing starting in the tent behind us, but the violin player persevered and there was an urgency about his delivery that made me think he welcomed this opportunity to pass the story on. He began by saying his violin was a 'church instrument', specially made at the beginning of the eighteenth century for a musician in an Italian church orchestra. Every well-endowed church in Italy had its own orchestra by the mid-seventeenth century, when violin music was already so popular that the demand for instruments was almost insatiable. He said somebody in the Church must have had the bright idea of solving this problem by going to Cremona and placing bulk orders with luthiers there, and I remember enjoying the idea of those church officials on their ecclesiastical spending spree.

A violin is usually signed on a label stuck to the inside of the back, where it can be seen through one of the f-shaped holes in its belly. But you could squint through the f-hole in the belly of Lev's old violin for as long as you liked without seeing anything at all. You might think the label had fallen off, as sometimes happens, but its owner explained it had never been there at all, because none of those church instruments were ever signed. Apparently this was a ruse for controlling the value of all the violins the Church commissioned. A signed instrument made by a well-known luthier would have increased in value year on year, so that parish priests, bishops and cardinals might have become some of the most successful violin dealers in the world. By insisting that the instruments were unsigned, the Church avoided the embarrassment of corrupting its officials, while keeping tight control over the value of its instruments. Why would talented luthiers in Cremona agree to such a dubious arrangement? Because the Church was also expert in temptation, and while protecting the probity of its own officers it enticed luthiers to produce a rapid flow of unsigned instruments in return for a tax-free income. According to the owner of Lev's violin, the promise of exceptional profits seduced even the more distinguished violin makers.

Unlabelled and anonymous, those church violins stood outside any kind of value system. They had no financial worth, and yet of all the changes wrought by the violin family on Italian culture, one of the most dramatic was driven by them in churches all over the peninsula, where they worked their voices into the form and fabric of the liturgy in ways that would change it for ever. This process was well underway by the mid-seventeenth century, when the new potential of violins from Cremona had already inspired forms of music that were gradually transforming the whole experience of going to church. Violin concertos and sonatas had been inserted into the liturgy as preludes and interludes to the sung sections in services, chants had been replaced by violin music, and when Mass was celebrated in a well-endowed church, the congregation often enjoyed a solemn, soft-toned violin concerto during the elevation of the host, a meditative violin sonata during Communion and a series of concerti grossi for strings between Bible readings. Much of this innovation was triggered from inside the Church, because bishops, popes and cardinals were some of the most generous patrons of new music in Italy.

Violin players and player-composers flocked to Milan, Bologna, Venice, Rome and Naples to seek work in cathedrals, pilgrimage churches, monasteries and convents. Although a job with an opera orchestra was better paid than church work, contracts were for one season only, whereas a post as *maestro di cappella*, or as a violinist in a church orchestra, could be a job for life. In some places, such as the basilica of San Marco in Venice, violin players' positions were handed down from father to son. This was a wonderful arrangement for the family involved, but made it almost impossible for outsiders to find work.* Violinists also found jobs in the courts of cardinals, bishops and other princes of the Church, and of all the players who made their living in this way the most important was Arcangelo Corelli. Virtuoso, composer and teacher, he dominated the musical life of his generation, and stoked up passion for violins and their music all over Europe.

Corelli was born in 1653 in a small town close to Ravenna, in the Emilia-Romagna region of northern Italy, and like so many children of his generation, he probably had his first violin lessons with the local priest. He certainly continued his training in Bologna, which was celebrated as a centre of violin culture in those days. When he was twenty-two he moved to Rome, and spent most of the next decade building up his reputation as a freelance violinist by playing the oratorios and concerti grossi performed by church orchestras all over the city. In this way he got to know the composers whose works he performed, as well as attracting the attention of some of the city's most generous patrons. By 1679 he had joined the court of the exiled Queen Christina of Sweden, and was composing sonatas for the musical *accademie* at her palace. In the mid-1680s he

* Eleanor Selfridge Field, 'Venice in an Era of Political Decline', in G. J. Buelow (ed.), *The Late Baroque Era, Man & Music*, Palgrave Macmillan, 1993, p. 74.

composed, performed and organized musical events at the court of Cardinal Benedetto Pamphili, and when Pamphili left Rome in 1690 Corelli soon found a new patron in Cardinal Pietro Ottoboni, the young nephew of Pope Alexander VIII. Ottoboni appointed Corelli court musician, or *musico*, gave him a job for life and an apartment in his palace.

Never mind the success of the Amati, Guarneri, or even Stradivari himself, no luthier ever sat for a portrait in Cremona. But Corelli belonged to a different class. He mixed with his patrons like a friend, and often had his portrait painted. All these images convey a man with wide-set eyes and a gentle, pleasant expression. But with a violin in hand he was transformed. He gave virtuoso performances all over Europe, and the historian and musicologist François Raguenet returned from one in France, shocked by Corelli's style of delivery. 'I never met with any man who suffered his passions to hurry him away so much whilst he was playing on the violin,' he said, 'as the famous Arcangelo Corelli, whose eyes will sometimes turn red as fire; his countenance will be distorted, his eyeballs roll as in an agony, and he gives in so much to what he is doing that he doth not look like the same man.'* Performances like this took Europe by storm, and brought the violin to the attention of an ever wider audience.

Corelli's job as a *musico* in the court of Cardinal Ottoboni was both glamorous and deeply practical. Composing or selecting music for every occasion on the Church calendar kept him in the public eye, feeding his fame in both Italy and abroad. However, it was also his remit to find musicians for every performance, arrange their transport, draw up their contracts, pay their wages, rehearse them, conduct them and play the violin alongside them.† Corelli was also famous for assembling the largest orchestras Rome had ever seen,

* David D. Boyden, *The History of Violin Playing from Its Origins to 1761*, Clarendon Press, 1965, p. 243.
† John Spitzer and Neal Zaslaw, *The Birth of the Orchestra: History of an Institution, 1650–1815*, Oxford University Press, 2005, p. 117.

stunning his audiences with a volume of sound they had never experienced before. When Ottoboni asked him to gather an orchestra for Alessandro Scarlatti's oratorio *Il regno di Maria assunta in cielo*, he appointed a hundred players, at least half of them violinists. A large stage with painted backdrops was built in the courtyard of his patron's city palace, Palazzo Cancelleria. Ottoboni invited his guests to arrive at dusk, when everything was already brilliantly illuminated by a magical combination of flaming torches, chandeliers and coloured lanterns. Their seats were in carriages that had been unhitched and arranged side by side like the boxes at a theatre. As soon as the performance began, the music of the violins and all the other instruments poured out into the street, just as it had done when I heard Lev's violin for the first time. The sound lured crowds of people, who did their best to get a glimpse of the performance beyond the palace gates.*

Corelli's protégés, both Italian and foreign, dominated musical life in Europe for a generation, and his solo and trio sonatas and concerti grossi were printed in foreign editions and performed everywhere. It was really Corelli who tied these forms down and created the archetypes that served as models for composers of violin music all over Europe. While I was reading about his career promoting the violin, I heard that one of his concerti grossi *da chiesa* was going to be performed in a cathedral not too far from my home. This was such a good opportunity to hear the music as Corelli intended that I bought a ticket at once, and now I really do understand why eighteenth-century churchgoers found his work so compelling. With Corelli there is no preamble, you just seem to happen upon a discussion already in full flow. And if you ever forget what the conversation is about, you can be sure the violins will remind you before long by returning to the theme. There was something truly ethereal about their sound as they busied themselves in the dim spaces of cupolas and vaulted ceilings, filling each crevice of the vast building with their voices.

* *Ibid.*, p. 122.

By the late seventeenth century the rich and fashionable people in musical cities such as Venice, Milan and Bologna had begun to attend church services in much the same way as they went to the opera. They didn't care if the concerto played to accompany the priest's business at the altar was so loud that it drowned out his voice. And if the sonata played during the offertory finished too soon, they assumed the orchestra would fill the gap with another one. Or if, as was just as likely, the music was too long, they expected the priest to wait patiently for it to end before continuing the business of the service, so that all in all violins and their music began to seem more important than the liturgy itself.

Some of the finest violin music in Europe could be heard in the churches and chapels attached to *ospedali* in Venice. There was an *ospedale* dedicated to resolving every kind of human calamity. Those afflicted by incurable diseases could go to the Ospedale degli Incurabili on the Zattere, the homeless were given shelter at the Ospedale dei Derelitti, close to the monastery of SS Giovanni e Paolo, and beggars were taken off the streets by the Ospedale dei Mendicanti in Castello. Mothers who were unmarried or unable to care for their babies could bundle them into the *scaffetta*, a crib-sized revolving drawer in the wall of the Ospedale della Pietà on the Riva dei Schiavoni. Of course the Pietà ran an orphanage, but most of the other *ospedali* also cared for orphans and foundlings, and made it part of their mission to train these children in useful trades. By the sixteenth century there was such demand for musicians from churches and theatres that music was considered a key skill, and the *ospedali* began to give any little girls who showed signs of musical talent a conservatoire training. At first they would be given lessons by the more senior pupils, but the *ospedali* also employed some of the most distinguished musicians and composers of the day as music teachers and *maestri di cappella*.

Antonio Vivaldi was only twenty-five when he was appointed violin teacher at the Ospedale della Pietà in 1703, with special responsibility for acquiring new instruments for the girls' orchestra. And he soon doubled his salary by taking on viola teaching as well.* By 1716 Vivaldi was both musical director of La Pietà and a European celebrity. Nobody could have expected orphans at the Pietà to pay for their own instruments, and so it struck me that the Church might have commissioned their violins as the owner of Lev's violin had described, offering a good tax-free income to anyone who would agree to produce them at top speed and leave them unsigned. His story had been so sparse that I began to explore this idea in the hope of making it more substantial. What if Lev's violin had been sent from Cremona to Venice as soon as the varnish dried on its brand-new body? And what if it had been given to an orphan child at the beginning of her musical training at the Ospedale della Pietà? Through constant practice and a conservatoire culture of excellence, that little girl would eventually have developed the skills she needed to join the church orchestra, where she would continue to improve by performing as many as forty memorial Masses in a day on Lev's violin, not to mention the regular concerts given for visitors.

The *ospedali* orchestras were all permanent institutions with plenty of time for rehearsals, and this set them apart from other orchestras in the city. Vivaldi worked the girls like professionals at the Pietà, and while his music was making him famous, it would also have been teaching Lev's violin to speak as if it really had something to say, seeping into the fabric of its belly and feeding into the voice it was just beginning to develop. I found myself imagining it among a jostling crowd of girls whispering in the vestry before Vespers. 'Have you taken my music?' 'I'm hungry.' 'You're standing on my foot.' They would all be in the red dresses with lace collars that they wore only for performances, and if the service was especially long or important they would all have been given an extra portion of supper. When Vivaldi appeared at the vestry door, the girls would fall into line and move out into the candlelit nave of the church. Silent and almost invisible in their dark uniforms, they

* Denis Arnold, 'Orphans and Ladies', *Proceedings of the Royal Musical Association*, 89th Sess. (1962–3), pp. 31–47, 35.

parted like a stream into four tributaries. The choir would have to climb narrow staircases to lofts that faced each other across the candlelit space, and the girl carrying Lev's violin would go with half of the orchestra to sit beside one of the church organs.

I imagined the doors of the church opening on to a canal, so that an evening breeze smelling of sewage and salt, bad fish and good cooking could blow in, bothering the candles and billowing the black muslin curtains that concealed both singers and musicians from the congregation. Then someone would shut the doors, and the only smells would be of incense and burning beeswax candles. The congregation would gasp as the invisible choir and orchestra flooded the chancel with music that was surprisingly worldly and brilliant. It filled the great space like a second structure, a vast new architecture of music that made the actual liturgy seem almost incidental. Then came the sound of zecchini, livres, scudi, gulden, florins, lire, gold sovereigns and schillings, currencies from all over Italy and Europe, tumbling on to the offering plates, as if the girls were milkmaids, filling buckets with the warm coins that would eventually be paid out again in their dowries.

There are many first-hand accounts of services in the churches of the *ospedali*. Some of the congregation went specifically to hear the music, and some were drawn almost as much by the idea of a gathering of so many beautiful young women. Jean-Jacques Rousseau was one of these. He was vexed by the curtains and iron grills concealing the faces of those 'angels', and with 'not an idea of anything so voluptuous and affecting as this music; the richness of the art, the exquisite taste of the vocal part, the excellence of the voices, the justness of the execution', he became obsessed by the idea of seeing them properly.* Eventually he wangled an invitation to lunch from a friend on the board at the Ospedale dei Mendicanti. Here he was introduced to Sophia, who 'was horrid', Cattina, who 'had but one eye', and Bettina, who was 'entirely disfigured' by smallpox. So much for angels, and yet Rousseau realized that they could not

---

* Jean-Jacques Rousseau, *Confessions*, https://bit.ly/2KZgoiy

make music as they did 'without intelligence and sensibility', and by the time he left the house, he was 'almost in love with each of these ugly faces'.

She may have arrived at the *ospedale* as something spurned, a damp baby in a bundle of blankets, but after years of training, an abandoned child with a worthless church violin could change her social standing entirely. Take Maddalena Lombardini. As the daughter of an impoverished family she had no prospects, and yet after graduating from the Ospedale dei Mendicanti in 1767 she would become one of the first female violin virtuosi in the world. Many girls' prospects were transformed in this way, and when I thought about this, it struck me that although people make things, things are very often the making of people.

Mood Music

The Lives of Church Violins and Their Musicians

What would life have been like for a violin in a church orchestra? When I asked this question I found myself suddenly remembering a strange experience in Padua years ago. It was a hot morning and coaches were prowling the side streets as usual, disgorging passengers wherever they could escape the notice of the traffic police. As soon as their feet touched the pavement, busloads of tourists advanced in small battalions towards the piazza in front of the Basilica di Sant' Antonio. The morning sun was heating up the streets, and in the piazza there were already noisy crowds around stalls selling St Anthony's face emblazoned on fridge magnets and postcards. I turned my back on all of them and pushed open the door of the Basilica. I can still remember the moment it shut, and the cool silence that closed over me. I had come inside to take refuge from the crowds, and yet I soon realized that the enormous incense-drenched silence was already inhabited by hundreds and hundreds of people. They had formed a queue that stretched the length and breadth of the building, and you only had to glance at it to know there was no prospect of barging in.

When I look back over years of slipping into churches in Italy, I realize I've always had a tendency to join queues, even when I don't know what is at the end of them, and this wasn't the first time it had landed me in deep trouble. Many years before I had blundered into a side chapel at San Marco in Venice, looking for a private place to cry about some unrequited teenage passion. There was a queue on that occasion too, and I remember joining it almost automatically, probably sniffing noisily. I am still too embarrassed to tell you what

64

happened when I realized I was queuing to take Mass with close family at a memorial service, or how I managed to escape the family reunion afterwards. And yet there I was again, taking my place in an ecclesiastical queue, as ignorant as ever. And after an obedient half hour I discovered what I had been waiting for, because by then I was first in line to kiss St Anthony's tongue. This all made more sense to me later, when I found out that St Anthony had been a mesmerizing preacher who died in 1231. Initially he was buried in an unimportant local church in Padua, but as soon as the new basilica was completed thirty years later, they dug him up again and reburied him. That's when the miracle was revealed, for although his body had decomposed as expected, the tongue that had shaped and delivered all those sermons was as pink and moist as ever. Eventually time must have taken its natural toll on the vaguely tongue-shaped object under the glass dome of the reliquary, turning it tawny and crenellating its edges, so that it looked like a lumpy land mass in a sea of gold.

My moment at the front of the queue came and went in seconds. I could have genuflected and stooped to kiss that sacred object, just like everyone else, but instead I shuffled past and then bolted out of the door to rejoin the modern world. Looking back, I wish I had paused to place my kiss among all the other smeary kisses on the glass of the reliquary, for in that moment present and past would have met, as it did for everyone whose kisses closed the 750-year gap between St Antony's life and their own. My kiss wouldn't have been for St Anthony though. In retrospect, it would have been for the visceral connection of lip contact with a past that put violins at the heart of religion, and gave them power to change what they found there.

The music of Lev's violin in a church orchestra would have been just one strand in a huge, rich, colourful, lethargic style of worship, a performance that doused all five senses with a cocktail of sounds, sights and scents, beautiful shapes and colours, unique tastes and textures. Worship had been this full-body experience in Italy ever since the Middle Ages when, instead of being considered very earthly distractions as they might be today, all the senses were invested with religious significance and perceived as tools for grasping abstract spiritual concepts, describing spiritual experience and reaching a better understanding of the divine. You might expect the role of the senses to have diminished by the time Lev's violin was indentured to the Church at the beginning of the eighteenth century, when Enlightenment philosophers all over Europe were promoting a more rational and scientific approach to life. However, early eighteenth-century Italy was suspended in a time warp, and as the historian Giuliano Procacci put it, even Rome, with its Classical ruins and crowds of priests and beggars, 'seemed to embody the antithesis of all that a "civilised" society should have been, in the eyes of enlightened eighteenth-century opinion'.* If the Vatican and the Papal States were so far behind the times, it is not surprising that churches all over the Italian peninsula were immune to change, their old-fashioned, sensory style of worship uninterrupted by any awkward new philosophies.

The only way for the Church to harness the senses to religious worship was through material objects, and so it didn't matter if a violin belonged to the modest ensemble of a small parish or the orchestra of a huge monastic institution – it would always have been part of a large community of things. There were lots of other instruments in the orchestra, of course, and they all lived alongside precious and beautifully crafted utensils used during the celebration of Mass and other church rituals, textiles for making altar cloths and vestments, and paintings, sculptures, mosaics, bibles, prayer books, tables and other pieces of furniture. Charles Dickens visited San Marco in the mid-nineteenth century, and his description of its interior is still valid today. He found the basilica '. . . golden with old mosaics, redolent of perfumes; dim with the smoke of incense; costly in treasures of precious stones and metals, glittering through iron bars; holy with the bodies of deceased saints; rainbow-hued with windows of stained glass; dark with carved woods and coloured marbles; obscure in its vast heights, and lengthened distances; shining with silver lamps and winking lights; unreal, fantastic

---

* Giuliano Procacci, *The History of the Italian People*, Penguin, 1978, p. 248.

solemn, inconceivable throughout'.* Stage-managing great impressions like this has always made the Church a consumer on a grand scale, and during the Counter-Reformation it turned congregations into consumers too, by giving everyone personal responsibility for their own acts of devotion. This obliged them to buy the physical props such as rosaries, relics, prayer books, religious pictures and crucifixes, which were thought to help them pray. And once lured into the marketplace in this way, it is said that people were often tempted to buy secular goods as well, so that some historians even suggest that the Church created the first generation of consumers, and they name Christianity as one of the main triggers of modern capitalism in the West.†

I searched for a paper trail to confirm my fantasy about Vivaldi going to Cremona to find violins for his pupils at the Ospedale della Pietà, but it turned out that all of the instruments he commissioned were made in Venice. Of course they were. This was a much more practical solution than going all the way to Cremona when Venice already had so many esteemed luthiers of its own. And the Church certainly was practical when it came to getting items on its shopping list. Whether it needed incense, amber, candles or violins, it waited calmly for the market to respond to its demands. When Italy had run short of beeswax for making candles in the Middle Ages, for example, the Church simply bided its time. Eventually merchants in Genoa and Venice spotted this new opportunity, and set off for unpopulated regions of Russia and eastern Europe, where there would always be more beeswax than the scattered population could use.‡ And then there was the amber used for making rosaries and reliquaries, candlesticks, incense and lamps. The upper classes were always the Church's main competitor. They used

---

* Charles Dickens, *Pictures from Italy*, Bradbury and Evans, 1846, p. 112.
† Cissie Fairchilds, 'Marketing the Counter Reformation', in *Visions and Revisions of Eighteenth-Century France*, ed. C. Adams et al., Penn State Press, 2005.
‡ Peter Spufford, *Power and Profit: The Merchant in Medieval Europe*, Thames & Hudson, 2006.

beeswax candles to light their houses, and amber for buttons, jewellery and even perfume made from ground amber.* There were Baltic amber merchants in Venice, but they could never hope to meet the demand from their fashionable customers and the Church.† Once again, however, the Church only had to wait until the exorbitant prices fetched by Baltic amber inspired Italian farmers and fishermen to pay more attention to the riches all around them. Then the market was flooded with amber from the sea off Sicily, from the mountains near Bologna, from the insides of limestone rocks in Umbria, and in fields near Ancona.‡

What about the insatiable demand for violins to play in ecclesiastical orchestras? The Church was in hot competition again, this time with theatres and impresarios gathering instruments for a multitude of well-funded opera orchestras. And despite the special commissioning of church violins, this problem would eventually resolve itself as well, when a rash of new lutherie workshops sprang up during the seventeenth century in Mantua, Ferrara, Milan, Venice and other towns and cities all over northern Italy. Who knows, perhaps the Church offered its tax-free inducements to luthiers in those cities as well.

The music of Lev's violin became part of an all-encompassing synaesthetic experience when brought together with beeswax candles, amber rosaries, and all the other objects that shaped and intensified church worship. Its power depended in part upon the contrast between two environments, the secular and the sacred. I still remember leaving the over-heated, over-busy streets of Padua behind when I blundered into the basilica, and the cool silence of its

* Rachel King, 'The Beads with which we Pray are Made of It', in Wietse de Boer and Christine Göttler, *Religion and the Senses in Early Modern Europe*, Brill, 2013, p. 165.
† Rachel King, 'Whose Amber? Changing Notions of Amber's Geographical Origin', National Museums Scotland, Ostblick, no. 2, 2014, vol. v, 1618–1801.
‡ Rachel King, 'Finding the Divine Falernian', *V&A Online Journal*, Issue no. 5, Autumn 2013, ISSN 2043-667X. https://bit.ly/2BTeo8p

interior. Outside the weather would always go on pleasing or assaulting the senses, but the basilica had its own weather system and landscape, where the walls of the vast building loomed like distant hills, the air was always still, light was coloured and diffused by stained glass, and candles ensured that darkness never really fell. On their way to Sant' Antonio, the congregation used to walk through a continuous flux of smells, many too strong, too dangerous or startlingly unpleasant to be tolerated in Italian cities today. Stepping over the threshold meant exchanging this extraordinary pungency for the smell of beeswax candles overlaid by the heavenly perfume of burning incense made from exotic resins, gums and spices. But of all the sensations encompassed by church worship, sound was the most important. Leonardo da Vinci summed up its qualities in a brief observation about hearing. 'As it is born,' he wrote, 'so it dies, and it is as fleeting in its death as it is in its birth.' And yet despite its transience, the music Lev's violin delivered was one of the most important elements of religious experience.

Violins and their close relations had been playing an ever more dominant role in church worship since the mid-sixteenth century, and this put them at the heart of musical culture at a time when Italy was the musical centre of Europe, Italian was the international language of music and Italian church music inspired composers everywhere. However, it also pitched them into a debate that had been raging ever since the Council of Trent met for the last time in 1563, scrutinized the character of church music and declared that it should not have anything 'lascivious', 'impure' or 'secular' about it.* It is almost impossible to overestimate the confusion these three words caused during the seventeenth and early eighteenth centuries, for, while it was obliged to uphold the Council of Trent's stipulations, the Church also wanted to be a source of music so uplifting and compelling that it would attract huge congregations,

---

* K. G. Fellerer and Moses Hadas, 'Church Music and the Council of Trent', *The Musical Quarterly*, vol. 39, no. 4 (October 1953), pp. 576–7.

fill them with spiritual feeling and a sense of the glory of God, and encourage them to give generously when the collection plate did its rounds.

This was the conflict, and violins were always at the heart of it because their voices now dominated church music. Each new pope must have been daunted by the prospect of trying to preserve the purity of worship, and during the seventeenth century many of them tried their best to control music through a series of encyclicals. These were serious bits of legislation, and any *maestro di cappella* who contravened them could face a lifelong ban from working as a professional musician, a sizeable fine (payable in part to the person who had reported him), and a real possibility of imprisonment.

Things were still much the same when Cardinal Ottoboni's uncle, Pope Alexander VIII, died in 1691. The usual conclave of cardinals gathered to select a new pope, and Cardinal Ottoboni, who was not a member of the conclave on that occasion, asked his *musico*, Arcangelo Corelli, to entertain his colleagues by performing a *bellissima serenata* just outside the walls of the Vatican. Taking a choir, six violin players, two violas, two viols and a lute with him, Corelli went straight to the Cortile del Belvedere and began to play. The marshal of the conclave stuck his head out of a small window as soon as he heard them. What happened next encapsulates the offence that music still caused. Outraged by the performance of secular music so close to the boundary of the Holy See, the marshal said he would have had them all thrown in prison if he had known what they planned to do. Other cardinals flung open windows and pelted everyone with stones, injuring one of the musicians so badly that he couldn't walk away unaided.*

Disagreements about church music rumbled on into the eighteenth century, and it was not until 1749 that Pope Benedict XIV conceded in these rather offensive terms that music '. . . may be

---

* John Spitzer and Neal Zaslaw, *The Birth of the Orchestra: History of an Institution, 1650–1815*, Oxford University Press, 2005, p. 118.

tolerated as long as it is serious and does not because of its length
cause boredom or serious inconvenience to those in the choir, or
the celebrants at the altar during Vespers and Mass'.* The pope also
tried to resolve the increasingly uncomfortable similarities between
sacred and secular music by stipulating that a church ensemble must
be very different from the kind of orchestra you would expect to
find at the opera. To this end, certain 'warlike' instruments should
be excluded from church. Violins were never on this hit list, and in
practice, the lack of names for modern instruments in the pope's
neo-Latin made it difficult for anyone to know exactly which ones
he was referring to, although drums, horns and trumpets were
certainly banned.†

When it came to finding out about the path that Lev's violin
might have taken in the wake of these troubled times, Charles Burney was a rich resource. He was an eighteenth-century violin
player, a music teacher and the author of a great tome entitled *A
General History of Music*, which encompassed the music of Britain,
Holland, Germany, France and Italy. Other writers might have
been content to reiterate received wisdom about musical life on
the continent, but he was determined to form his own opinions
from first-hand experience. In 1770 he set off to gather all the information he needed in France and Italy, taking his own food,
saucepans and bedding with him, as well as a small library, printed
copies of a 'plan' for his *General History* translated into several languages, a sword, a brace of pistols and letters of introduction to all
the most important Italian musicians, composers, patrons and pro-
fessors.‡ The following year he published his travel journal, calling
it *The Present State of Music In France and Italy*. The world had to
wait a little longer for his *General History*, which came out in four
volumes between 1776 and 1789.

* *Ibid.*, p. 160.
† Michael Talbot, *The Sacred Vocal Music of Antonio Vivaldi*, L. S. Olschki, 1995, p. 61.
‡ Paul Henry Lang, 'Tales of a Travelling Musical Historian', *The Journal of Musicology*, vol. 2, no. 2 (Spring 1983), pp. 196–205.

As a violin player and teacher himself, Burney was especially interested in the training of violinists in Italy, and in the details of their working lives. When he visited the *ospedali* in Venice, which were some of the oldest music schools in Europe, he was particularly impressed by the girls of the Ospedale dei Mendicanti, who performed a concert in his honour. Many could play several instruments, 'and there seemed to be great decorum and good discipline observed in every particular; for these admirable performers, who are of different ages, all behaved with great propriety, and seemed to be well educated.'*

The Venetian *ospedali*'s recipe for education was so successful, and the demand for musicians so great, that by the middle of the seventeenth century four orphanages in Naples had transformed themselves into conservatoires for the boys in their care.† Burney heard some of these students play as well, and was mystified by their poor performance. All became clear, however, when he visited the Ospedale di Sant' Onofrio, where he found eight boys sitting on their beds in the dormitory while practising the harpsichord.‡ There were violinists trying to play at the same time, while other boys attempted to do their homework. Meanwhile a trumpet player was 'screaming upon his instrument till he was ready to burst' on the staircase outside, and a French horn was 'bellowing in the same manner'. Burney concluded that nobody at the Ospedale di Sant' Onofrio could concentrate enough to refine their technique, so that all in all he no longer had any trouble understanding 'the slovenly coarseness' of their public performances.§ Perhaps things were easier for the castrati among the students. They lived alone on the top floor, where the rooms were both quieter and

---

* Charles Burney, *The Present State of Music in France and Italy*, Elibron Classics, 2005, p. 184.
† David Schoenbaum, *The Violin: A Social History of the World's Most Versatile Instrument*, Norton, 2013, p. 289.
‡ Burney, *The Present State of Music in France and Italy*, p. 326.
§ *Ibid.*, pp. 325–6.

warmer, 'for fear of colds, which might not only render their delicate voices unfit for exercise at present, but hazard the entire loss of them forever'.*

Violin players who graduated successfully from Venice's *ospedali* sometimes continued their training. Maddalena Lombardini had spent eight years at the Ospedale dei Mendicanti learning composition, singing and violin, before she joined the school set up in 1728 by celebrated violin player and composer Giuseppe Tartini in Padua. He offered his students a two-year course in violin and composition. It was one of the first formal courses specifically designed for violin players, and Lombardini went on to become one of the first female virtuosi.† Tartini taught ten hours a day for forty years, attracting so many foreign students to his private conservatoire that it came to be known as The School of Nations.

Violin players who accepted a position in a church orchestra soon after completing their training could not expect to be well paid. Burney's explanation was that the salaries of church musicians had been static for many years. He blamed this on the opera, which offered enormous salaries to principal singers and musicians. Result? While church music 'falls into decay and goes from bad to worse . . . that of theatres receives daily improvements by additional rewards'. Burney even went so far as to remark that 'all the *musici* in the churches at present are made up of the refuse of the opera houses.'‡

Life was very different for the virtuoso players Burney met on his travels, who seemed to earn more by working less. At the Chapel Royal in Turin he met the violinist and composer Gaetano Pugnani, who was paid eighty guineas a year to perform solos, 'and those just when he pleased'. Even so, Pugnani didn't appear to be putting much effort into his performance, but that was hardly surprising 'as

---

* *Ibid.*, p. 327.

† Toby Faber, *Stradivarius: Five Violins, One Cello and a Genius*, Macmillan, 2004, p. 72.

‡ Burney, *The Present State of Music in France and Italy*, pp. 273 and 303.

neither his Sardinian majesty, nor any one of the numerous royal family, seem to pay much attention to music'.* Italian virtuosi were utterly cosmopolitan. Pugnani had just returned from a triumphant three-year stint in London when Burney met him, and Giovanni Piantanida, whom Burney saw playing during a morning Mass in Bologna, had spent four years in England, where he published six violin sonatas and sometimes performed with Handel.

Stringed instruments dominated church orchestras all over Italy. Even on the most ordinary occasion there were forty musicians in the choir and orchestra at Basilica di Sant' Antonio in Padua, of which half were string players.† These musicians were accommodated in organ lofts suspended high above the ground on either side of the immense building, so that the choirs answered and echoed each other across the vast chancel. The standard of music varied enormously from church to church. Burney always wrote notes in his diary immediately after leaving a service, creating a fresh, honest and unsparing account of everything he heard. Despite its glowing reputation abroad, not all Italian music was good. Burney warned that unless you went to church during a festival or on a saint's day, you were likely to hear music 'as grave as that of our church services of two hundred years standing'. The congregations for these services were made up of 'clergy, trades-people, mechanics, country clowns, and beggars', who, Burney said, were 'very inattentive and restless, seldom remaining in church during the whole performance'.

I would have felt quite at home among these congregations, because I knew so little about music when I heard Lev's violin for the first time. We all invent excuses for our own ignorance, and when it came to music, I liked to blame this void on my upbringing. Although my father was always said to be a musical man, we only heard classical music when I was a child if we got up especially early and went to the cowshed. That's where we'd find him milking, one

* *Ibid.*, p. 72.
† *Ibid.*, pp. 129–30.

ear buried in a cow's warm flank, the other alert to the two-tone spurt and splash of milk in the bucket at his feet. Or perhaps not, because the enormous Bakelite radio on the dusty shelf above his head was always playing BBC Radio 3 at top volume, so that I came to associate all classical music with early mornings, the fug and jostle of cows and the pungency of fresh milk. Back in the house the only music I heard belonged to my brother. We had adjoining rooms, and by the time I was ten and he twelve I had heard Jimi Hendrix through my bedroom wall for the first time. And the second. And again and again and again. And that's the second-hand way I first listened to Dylan as well, and all the other things that formed his nascent musical taste. Of course I would eventually build up a soundtrack for my own life, but I never managed to shake off the sense of exclusion I had as a child in my bedroom, listening to those muffled sounds, as if music were a members-only club I would never be good enough to join.

When I heard Lev's violin play for the first time, it seemed to speak directly to me and deliver a deeply personal message. And now I began to fill my days with the joyful sounds of Corelli, San Martini, Galuppi, Vivaldi, Burney's great hero Giuseppe Tartini, and all the other composers whose music Burney would describe as 'pure', 'rich' or 'grateful'. As weeks of listening turned into months, I began to hear and be absorbed and involved in music in a way I had never experienced before. I expect it had as much to do with confidence as anything else, but whatever the cause, it means that I have burst through the doors of the music club and I am a full member now, for ever on the right side of the wall.

Political Instruments

Violins at the Medici Court in Florence

Violins were destined to be worked to the bone in eighteenth-century Italy. Some were employed by the Church, like Lev's violin, and others had jobs in the court orchestras and ensembles of petty states and kingdoms all over the peninsula. Cremona violins were still considered the best in the world, and so it is no surprise that many began their careers in the service of a king, queen or duke.

The Medici family, who ruled Florence for hundreds of years, amassed one of the greatest instrument collections in Italy between the sixteenth and eighteenth centuries. If you want to see what remains of this aristocratic family, all you have to do is walk up Via Ricasoli as I did, join the queue that will be snaking back towards the Duomo and wait your turn to go into the Galleria dell' Accademia. A thin autumn drizzle was falling when I went, so I was glad of the man touting umbrellas, and even gladder of the bar making its fortune from disappointed optimists like me. We must all have thought that skipping breakfast would secure us a place at the front of the queue, but instead we stood in line for an hour or more, sipping coffee from plastic cups and eating *cornetti* filled with unmanageable quantities of apricot jam. When it was time to go inside at last, and everyone else surged out of the booking hall and headed straight for the room where Michelangelo's sculpture of *David* lives like a convict, forever surrounded by guards, I walked away down an empty corridor to rooms that house what remains of the vast instrument collection created by generations of Medici grand dukes.

Of course there were Stradivarius instruments in the Medici orchestra, because Stradivari creamed off all the best customers for

Cremona violins. He couldn't help it. In 1684 a local marquis called Bartolomeo Ariberti commissioned him to make two violins and a cello as a present for Florence's Grand Prince Ferdinando II de' Medici. This was a wonderful commission because, unlike the Savoy princes in Turin, who seemed to employ virtuosi and famous composers out of a dreary sense of duty, Ferdinando had a genuine interest in music. He was a good singer and musician himself, and played the cello, the harpsichord, and eventually the piano, invented under his patronage by Bartolomeo Cristofori. Ferdinando was already taking such a serious interest in music by the time he was sixteen that he arranged for an opera called *Colla forza di Amore si vince Amore* ('Love is Won by the Strength of Love') to be performed in the family's country villa at Pratolino. His taste was never provincial, and he was already knowledgeable enough in his twenties to strike up a lasting friendship with Handel, whom he invited to Florence. Handel admired the work of Antonio Salvi, the Medici court physician and poet, so much that he engaged him to write the libretti for operas including *Ariodante*, *Rodelinda* and *Arminio,* which seemed to place Ferdinando at the heart of Handel's operatic career. Ferdinando also exchanged letters with Alessandro Scarlatti, who would write five operas for him, and staged his own opera season every year in the theatre built for him at Pratolino. He was involved in every aspect of these productions, selecting the librettists himself, telling the composers exactly how they should set texts to music, and choosing singers and musicians to deliver it. What a nightmare he must have been for everyone involved.

The opera season absorbed Ferdinando throughout July and August, and then he spent the rest of the year hosting private concerts in his own apartments at the Pitti Palace. He was also a great impresario of musical productions at Florence's Teatro della Pergola, and of magnificent entertainments in the streets and piazzas of the city, so that during his lifetime Florence became one of the most vibrantly musical cities in Europe. The Medici instrument collection had been at its largest during the 1620s. However, Ferdinando was as passionate about musical instruments as he was about music, and, as his life coincided with those of both Nicolò Amati and Stradivari in Cremona, the quality of the instruments in the collection under his care would never be surpassed.

This would be the unique and demanding setting for the lives of Stradivari's instruments, and perhaps that is why he took such a long time to deliver them. Six years after the commission, Ariberti finally received a heartfelt thank-you letter from the Grand Prince. Reporting back to Stradivari, Ariberti told him the musicians in the Medici court orchestra all thought his instruments 'quite perfect', and said they had 'never heard a violoncello with such an agreeable tone . . .' He signed off by saying 'I now have to request you to begin at once two violas, one tenor and the other contralto, which are wanted to complete the concerto.'*

So many of Stradivari's instruments have travelled the world that there is something extraordinary about being able to go to Florence and find the cello from the first commission and the tenor viola from the second still living in the heart of the city. The tenor viola has such delicate f-holes in its gleaming, russet belly, and such a beautifully carved scroll, that it is a perpetual statement of Stradivari's mastery of his craft. It is the only Stradivarius in the world that has never undergone the standard alterations inflicted on his other instruments over the centuries. The fingerboards on most of them have been replaced with the longer ones that enabled players to reach the high notes demanded by a classical repertoire. Not this viola. It still had Stradivari's original fingerboard, inlaid with the Medici coat of arms in glamorous mother-of-pearl. The tailpiece was original too, inlaid this time with a jaunty cupid drawing his bow. Stradivari's pen and ink drawings for these decorations are preserved in Cremona, with a note in his own writing identifying them as 'coats-of-arms I made to go on instruments for the Grand Prince of Tuscany'. Even the bridge, surely one of the most transient pieces of any

* From the original letter reproduced in an article by Alessandra Barabaschi in Tarisio's Cozio archive (https://bit.ly/2HU88zC). Stradivari made two more instruments at a later date, creating a quintet.

instrument, had survived, with Stradivari's inked-on pattern of flowers and leaves on one side and two colossi on the other.

Other violas, violins and cellos were the real labourers at court. Their taxing lifestyle meant they needed regular maintenance, repairs and alterations at the Medici workshop in the Uffizi, where there were up to a hundred highly talented instrument conservators and makers. However, repairs weren't always enough to send violins on their way. Musical fashions were constantly changing, and over the years court instruments had to endure minor ops and deep surgery to keep abreast of the times, so that their bodies were eventually transformed into palimpsests of European musical fashion, and of the technical innovations it demanded. The older instruments in the collection hadn't the projection to perform in a large space, or to be heard against the sound of a full orchestra, so they needed radical interventions if they were to keep their jobs at court. First they had to be opened up and given sturdier bass bars and sound posts to support increased pressure on their bellies and transmit vibrations more effectively. Then their necks had to be raised to increase the tension on the strings and make them produce a more penetrating sound. Even more serious surgery had been carried out on some instruments in the collection. Take the Nicolò Amati cello of 1650. Its strings were originally made from two strands of twisted animal gut. This meant that the lower strings were quite thick and a little bit stiff, and had to be a considerable length if they were to vibrate enough to produce low notes. Long strings meant a long body, and consequently Nicolò Amati's beautiful cello had always been a bit awkward to play. Towards the end of the seventeenth century, however, string-makers began lining the gut strings for cellos with a very thin wrapping of silver wire, meaning that they could be shorter and thinner without compromising the quality of the low notes.* You might think this would make old-fashioned cellos with their overgrown bodies redundant. Think again. Some skilled luthier in the Medici workshop simply reduced

* Gabriele Rossi Rognone (ed.), *Strumenti musicali, guida alle collezione medicee e lorenesi*, Galleria dell'Academia, Giunti, 2018, p. 327.

the length of Amati's cello, removed fillets of wood from the centre of its belly and back to make it narrower, and then re-strung it with a revolutionary 'overspun' G string.

When I consider what had been done to Nicolò Amati's cello, it reminds me of costumes I once saw designed by Léon Bakst for Sergei Diaghilev's Ballets Russes. They were about to be sold at auction, but in the meantime they were hanging on a rail in a friend's kitchen, filling the room with lush colour and dynamic shapes. I will forever ask myself what stopped me from trying on one of the costumes for the harem in *Scheherazade*, which were so suggestive and exotic that they seemed to reinterpret the human body. Instead, I went in among them all and admired expert alterations made over the years, adjustments that meant they could be used again and again by dancers in the casts of many different productions. They had been darned and patched in the most intimate places, and were so stained by sweat that it struck me they were probably impregnated with the DNA of some of the greatest dancers of the twentieth century. Some of these stars had even scrawled their names on the linings of their costumes – a practical precaution against mistakes in the hectic scramble of the dressing room.

Just like the instruments in the Accademia, Bakst's costumes were never meant to be seen in that static way. He conceived each one as part of a whirling mass of moving colour, made up of multiple costumes and an extraordinarily vivid set. They were all that is left of the magic of these productions, just as the instruments in the Medici collection are all that is left of the music that filled the Florentine court from the sixteenth to the nineteenth century. And like those costumes, the violins, violas, cellos and double basses were constantly adjusted and updated for new players and new repertoires. These days they are as dumb as *David* in the gallery next door, but from the sixteenth century until the dissolution of the Florentine court in 1861 they would rarely have been silent. Living at the heart of a vast network of relationships between the Medici, their subjects and their rivals at home and abroad, they performed all the music ever played at court, in the gardens of the family's country villas and city palaces, in their chapels and churches, and in the streets, theatres and piazzas of Florence. They were front-line soldiers in the Medici battle to be best among all the courts of Italy at entertaining foreign rulers and diplomats, best at dazzling their subjects and intimidating their rivals. Sometimes they worked to project a grandiose image, sometimes a fun-loving one, but *magnificenza* was always at the heart of their performance. They joined colourful processions through the streets of Florence, entertainments in the city's piazzas and in the grounds of its villas and palaces. They were the soloists during oratorios and festival Masses, and their music dazzled the audiences of plays and operas in ways that distracted them from the hardships of Medici rule. And it was a harsh life beyond the confines of court, for while Stradivari was making instruments for Ferdinando, his father Cosimo III de' Medici was taxing everyone and everything so harshly that Gilbert Burnet, Bishop of Salisbury, was shocked by the state of Florence when he visited the city in 1685. He found the countryside surrounding it 'so dispeopled that the soil in many places is quite neglected for want of hands to cultivate it; and in other places where there are more people, they look so poor and their houses are such miserable ruins, that it is scarce accountable how there should be so much poverty in so rich a country, which is all over full of beggars.'* Yet the voices of violins oiled the wheels of political negotiations, added a glimmer of joy to the sterile celebrations for inter-dynastic marriages and improved the atmosphere on countless other occasions. Sometimes the sounds encrypted in those worn old bodies are all we have left, because much of the music they played on these occasions was never preserved.

The role of violins and their players at court fell somewhere between that of a servant who could be summoned to work at any time of the day or night, and a close relation who was given access to the private heart of the family. They were often called on to play during a formal dinner at Palazzo Pitti, where Cosimo III was obsessed with promoting a vision of affluence. Apparently, 'no prince or ambassador

* *Bishop Burnet's Travels through France, Italy, Germany and Switzerland*, 1750.

came to Florence but was entertained with Oriental magnificence, and loaded with gifts on his departure. The banquets he gave for foreign visitors were legendary, the table laden with exotic food served by staff of every ethnic origin, all wearing their national costumes. Cosimo made a great spectacle of having fatted capons weighed at table. The violins playing table music would fall silent at this point, for if a brace failed to exceed twenty pounds Cosimo refused to eat, behaving as if their very appearance were a personal insult.'*

When they were not entertaining guests at dinner, some of the court violinists might be called on to supply little tunes during plays the Medici children performed for their mother, or take part in tender ceremonies celebrating the safe delivery of a new baby.† Others were given the job of playing soothing music in a sick room or even at a deathbed, and, like perfect guests, violins adapted their tone to all of these occasions.‡ These were the usual jobs musicians did in courts all over Italy, but you only have to look at the pictures hanging on the walls of the instrument gallery in the Accademia to know that things were going through a very different phase when Stradivari's instruments were shipped from Cremona to Florence in 1690. Rich with detail and colour, the paintings were made between 1685 and 1687 by Antonio Domenico Gabbiani. His patron was Grand Prince Ferdinando himself, who gazes out of a portrait hanging by the door of the gallery. He is surrounded by singers, composers and musicians, and it is quite clear from their poses and expressions that these people are not servants, but friends. Gabbiani gave the same scrupulous attention to instruments as people. The glint of the metal on the cello string is as striking as the musicians' gleaming curls and the play of light on their satin jackets. He also captured a dazed expression on each of the men's faces, as if we had pushed open the door of a practice room and interrupted a moment of deep concentration between the players.

---

* Harold Acton, *The Last Medici*, Cardinal, 1988, pp. 151–2.
† Suzanne G. Cusick, *Francesca Caccini at the Medici Court: Music and the Circulation of Power*, University of Chicago Press, 2009, p. 61.
‡ *Ibid.*, p. 63.

Gabbiani's portrait of Ferdinando tells us he was a handsome man before corpulence set in. He was the child of a disastrous marriage between Cosimo III de' Medici, his morose father, and his angry mother, Marguerite-Louise d'Orléans, who abandoned him when he was twelve years old and returned to Paris. In some respects the man in the painting seems to have turned out exactly as you would expect, a typical boy from a dysfunctional family with too much money and not enough to do. He surrounded himself with such hedonistic friends that it took a long time for Florence to forget one of their nights on the town, or their parties at Pratolino. However, Gabbiani's paintings also depict violins, violas and cellos inhabiting a world peopled by the musical stars who considered Ferdinando a friend. Two of the group portraits include the violinists Francesco and Antonio Veracini, father and son. Francesco, grandfather and teacher of the much more famous Francesco Maria Veracini, is one of the few musicians in Gabbiani's portraits who has not bothered to wear a wig. There are smile lines around his mouth, and the look in his eyes suggests that he sees something ridiculous in holding a stationary bow for ever across the strings of his silent violin. The Veracini generally worked for Ferdinando only during the opera season. For the rest of the year they were big figures in the musical world of the city, where there were sometimes as many as seven members of their family playing at the same performance. Local impresarios treated the lesser members of the family as interchangeable, and instead of using first names to distinguish them in musicians' rosters, they listed them only by surname and number.

Ferdinando had a soft spot for young men. A black boy with a beautiful face, a pearl in his ear and a parrot on his wrist hovers in the background of one of the portraits. The prince enjoyed the company of castrati, and history refuses to forget the day his tutor walked in on him kissing Petrillo, his crush. Standing next to him in the painting is Francesco de Castro. He is singing to the violin accompaniment of Martino Bitti, another of Ferdinando's favourites.

The voices of violins and castrati had begun their slow domination of Italian music together, at the end of the sixteenth century. At first they worked in church, where women were forbidden to sing in the choir, and the high parts had always been performed by young boys or men with falsetto voices. In 1589 Pope Sixtus V overturned this old tradition and introduced castrati into the choir of San Pietro in the Vatican. When Charles Burney visited Italy in 1770, he tried to find out where the operations were carried out on the castrati he saw performing 'in every great town throughout Italy'. In Milan he was told that they were done in Venice, in Venice they said Bologna, and so on, so that he soon realized 'the Italians are so ashamed of it, that in every province they transfer it to some other'. He was assured that the practice was forbidden by every conservatoire, and yet it was the conservatoires that judged the potential of a boy's voice, and then allowed his parents to take him home 'for this barbarous purpose'. The Church never sanctioned castration, and Burney found out that 'it was death by the laws to all those who perform the operation, and excommunication to every one concerned in it,' and yet he found castrati performing in churches all over the Italian peninsula.* By the time Gabbiani was painting Francesco de Castro at the end of the seventeenth century, castrati were already lords of the opera, and the richest, most sought after and virtuosic singers of the age. In return, they had to learn to live with the sterility, osteoporosis and stigma that were their life sentence.

Ferdinando died in 1703, ten years before his father Cosimo III, and this marked the beginning of the end for a collection that had showcased instruments by the finest luthiers in Cremona, and brought them to the attention of every foreign visitor to the Medici court. On his father's death in 1713, the title passed to Ferdinando's brother, Gian Gastone. He was childless when he died in 1737, and his sister Anna Maria de' Medici left a will bequeathing all the family property to Francis I, Duke of Lorraine. Her bequest was made on condition that none of their rich collections of paintings, sculptures, books, antiquities, natural curiosities, scientific instruments or

---

* Charles Burney, *The Present State of Music in France and Italy*, Elibron Classics, 2005, p. 303.

anything else at all should be removed from Florence. But this obligation does not seem to have applied to the instrument collection, for many of the violins kept at Palazzo Pitti went missing while the building was occupied by Austrian troops after Anna Maria's death in 1743.* Those that remained were poorly maintained, loaned out to musicians who never returned them, and even sold by the people who should have been playing them.

When Francis I inherited the Grand Dukedom, musical life at court ground to a halt because he chose to remain in Austria rather than coming to live in Florence. Everything changed for the better when Pietro Leopoldo succeeded his father in 1765 and moved to Florence with his family. However, he was Austrian through and through when it came to music, and so he preferred the sound of wind instruments and percussion to violins. This was a period of profound neglect for the stringed instruments in the collection. The rigorous regime of maintenance in the Uffizi workshops had kept them going for centuries, but now it broke down. Some violins limped on until they simply wore out, and others suffered critical injuries and were never repaired. In 1784 the First Violin player at court even took advantage of this new age of neglect to sell one of the Stradivarius instruments to an Irish musician.

Despite being diminished and poorly maintained, the string section of the court orchestra played on until 1861, when Unification finally silenced it by dissolving the Grand Duchy of Tuscany and all the other petty states and their self-serving courts.

As I left the Accademia and walked back towards the Duomo, I thought of the emotional impact made by the violins in the collection over successive generations, and it struck me that Italian violins have been leading people like me by their noses for centuries, defining their moods, talking to their imaginations, manipulating their thoughts, and even sending them whirling off on journeys like the one that was taking me all over Italy.

---

* Toby Faber, *Stradivarius: Five Violins, One Cello and a Genius*, Macmillan, 2004, pp. 155–6.

Cozio

The World's First Violin Collector and Connoisseur

You may remember that my first meeting with Lev's violin coincided with poignant weeks spent emptying my mother's house after she died, trying to recall the significance of every object she owned. Was that a painting of our house seen from a strange angle and a great distance? Or was that just what I imagined as a child, when every painting on the wall represented my small world in some way? Were these the little cardboard squares inscribed with letters my father used to teach me to read, or were they stand-ins on some long-defunct Scrabble board? Did the old pine corner cupboard come from my grandmother's home in Norway, or had my mother picked it up for nothing at a local auction? Without history or geography, these things were as anonymous as strangers, and now it was too late to hear their stories one more time, too late to know their secrets. And then there was Lev's violin. The owner had been told it was worthless, and yet the story clinging to it like mist gave it a value that would in my mind always outstrip its financial worth.

In those months I lived midstream in a steady flow of things issuing from the old house as we prepared to sell it, a deluge of objects I had known all my life. The polished sideboard with an inexplicably spicy smell in its cupboard and drawers; the table with the satisfying crack down its middle, where we used to put the tips of our knives and set them vibrating right down to the hilt; the rusty metal scoop for dishing out animal feed; the little cupboard where we put chipped plaster nativity figures at Christmas; the board games we played – although not very often; the books we read, the saucepans, coats, bicycles, binoculars, a lifetime's accumulation of things that seemed poised to lurch towards my own home on crippled legs, shouting 'We're all orphans now!' I was finding it impossible to choose which ones to take in. My siblings wanted none of it, but for me, each small separation had the power to make me miss my mother all over again. Her possessions were all that remained of a time and a place I had left long ago, and they provoked a kind of nostalgia that felt like the worst kind of homesickness.

I was an easy target for those swilling objects looking for new places to settle, and at first I was so hospitable that our house began to look as if some ancestral fly tipper had run riot in the night. We lived among the looming shadows of extra furniture, and got used to walking sideways towards our bedroom down an avenue of paintings stacked against the walls. Picking my way through this confusion, I sometimes thought of the clear-cut, brutal evaluation that had been made of Lev's violin – worthless – and then I wondered if the violin trade might have something to teach me about which of my mother's things to value, which to sell and which to give away.

These days violin dealing is a vast and international business, but if you trace it all the way back to its roots, you find just one person, an eighteen-year-old born in 1755 in a village in Piedmont called Casale Monferrato, which is about 150 kilometres upriver from Cremona on the Po. His magnificent name was Count Ignazio Alessandro Cozio di Salabue, and he had just inherited his father's fortune. With no duties beyond overseeing the family estate, he must have been casting around for a direction in life. His father had left him an Andrea Amati violin when he died, and perhaps this gave him a special interest in Cremona. It was less than forty years since Stradivari's death, and yet Cozio knew that the Cremona tradition of violin-making was already dying out. Some blame this on Stradivari. He dominated the trade, stealing all the business from lesser luthiers and forcing them to leave town in search of work, so that when his death was followed by that of Guarneri del Gesù in 1744, Carlo Bergonzi was the last luthier left in Cremona.

Stradivari's son Francesco left the contents of the family

workshop to his half-brother, Paolo, who was Stradivari's youngest son by his second marriage. In 1746 Paolo called on Carlo Bergonzi to bring the remaining stock into saleable condition. After less than two years, however, Bergonzi himself was dead, and this brought the golden age in Cremona to an abrupt end. It is said that by 1795, when Napoleon's army came marching through the city, there wasn't an old-master violin to be had in the city. How do we know? Because one of Napoleon's generals skived off to do a little shopping. He is said to have looked everywhere for an Amatius or a Stradivarius before rejoining his troops empty handed.

There must have been something about the dramatic decline of violin-making in Cremona that captured Cozio's imagination, for now he committed himself to preserving the tradition with all the passion of an adolescent. First he set about learning all there was to know about Cremona in the good old days by talking to anyone he could find still alive to remember it. Then he decided to build a reference collection of Cremona violins that could be used as a resource, as he put it, for understanding 'the secrets of this difficult art, so that they can be used again in Italy'.* If Cozio had set out on this mission alone, he would probably have been fleeced by wily old luthiers all over Italy. Fortunately he met Giovanni Battista Guadagnini, one of the finest luthiers of his generation, on a trip to Turin in 1773. Guadagnini may not have been entirely honest himself, however, for he allowed Cozio to believe that he was the protégé of one of Cremona's great workshops, when he was actually trained by his own father in Piacenza. Nevertheless, Guadagnini had a forty-year career behind him, he knew everyone in the business and they all knew him. Cozio commissioned him to buy both old instruments from Cremona and ones made by Italy's finest contemporary luthiers. He also committed to buying every instrument produced in Guadagnini's own workshop.

Cozio made a forensic examination of each new treasure that

* John Dilworth and Carlo Chiesa, 'Luigi Tarisio, part 1', Cozio Archive, 22 November 2017.

Guadagnini delivered, and in this way he built up an intimate knowledge of the working practices and styles of both the Cremonese masters and the best contemporary luthiers in Italy. He filled page after page with scribbled notes about the histories of all the instruments he handled, making meticulous observations about their appearances, design and dimensions. This gave him an instinct for the work of different masters that would make him into the world's first true connoisseur of violins and other stringed instruments.

A private income left Cozio with no need to earn money, and yet within a year of meeting Guadagnini he had started to deal in violins himself. It was not their financial worth that interested him, for his intentions were still altruistic. He saw dealing as a way of finding new instruments for his collection, and handling as many violins as possible to build up his expertise. Although he bought instruments made by luthiers from all over Italy, Cozio still valued violins from Cremona above all others, and when he heard that Paolo Stradivari was selling off the remaining instruments in his father's workshop, he was determined to buy the lot and add them to his collection. He also wanted to buy all of the artefacts Stradivari had used, including his tools, the forms he used for making violins, violas and cellos, and the notebooks in which he recorded the names of his customers. He chose not to meet Paolo Stradivari face to face, preferring to communicate through Guadagnini, or by letter. Cozio also got help from a dry-goods merchant in Turin called Giovanni Anselmi, as well as Pietro and Domenico Mantegazza, the first generation of a violin-making dynasty in Milan.* Using this small and disparate team as go-betweens, Cozio put persistent pressure on Paolo Stradivari, forever sending him messages about the unending list of things he was willing to buy. The letters preserved in Cremona's Biblioteca Statale show Paolo becoming increasingly irritable during the two-year negotiation. At one point

* David Schoenbaum, *The Violin: A Social History of the World's Most Versatile Instrument*, Norton, 2013, p. 150.

he committed wryly to ensuring that 'not a single thing belonging to my father be left in Cremona'.*

Every detail of Paolo Stradivari's transactions with Cozio is recorded, even the jar of delicious Cremonese *mostarda* made from candied fruit and mustard-spiced oil that Stradivari promised to throw in to sweeten the deal, and the name of the boatman who would ferry the goods up river to Casale Monferrato. In the end Paolo didn't even live to see the transaction completed, and it was his son, Antonio Stradivari II, who finalized the sale.

As well as Stradivari's tools and forms, Cozio bought some of the semi-transparent paper plans for the inlaid patterns on instrument bodies, as well as plans for violin cases and their latches, keyholes and hinges. And yet, despite all Cozio's efforts, some things had gone missing by the time the boat docked in Casale Monferrato. He was especially upset by the loss of the shop notebooks in which he believed 'there were various notes in logical order on instrument construction and a list of all the instruments made, plus a description of the persons to whom they were sold.' The stamp that Stradivari used to make labels – 'AS' and a circle enclosing a cross – was also missing, and so were the labels themselves. What a crushing disappointment this must have been for Cozio after waiting so long.

Cozio's close dealings with Guadagnini survived only until the sale went through in 1776. My guess is that Guadagnini was mortally offended when Cozio offered to lend him some of the forms from the Stradivari workshop, suggesting that they would help him to 'make violins more like Stradivari'.† Nevertheless, Cozio went on to a career lasting over fifty years, in which he handled many of the world's finest Guarneri, Stradivari and Amati violins, and kept a written record of them all. This *Carteggio*, as his papers are known, is also archived at the Biblioteca Statale in Cremona. Among the files is a sheaf of 300 pages dating from 1816, in which Cozio recorded

---

* Toby Faber, *Stradivarius: Five Violins, One Cello and a Genius*, Macmillan, 2004, p. 79.
† Schoenbaum, *The Violin*, p. 42.

all the instruments that ever passed through his hands, as well as some of the secrets from Cremona's old workshops. He was the first person to categorize Stradivari's instruments by the forms used to make them. He hadn't much time for neat writing, grammar, punctuation or spelling, and he tended to use dialect words instead of standard Italian. These were working notes, and so he would often cross things out, squeeze corrections between the lines and put additional comments and the names of his customers in the margins. Cozio's painstaking notes about the dimensions of instruments are equally confusing because he used an eccentric mix of different measuring systems. All this inconsistency makes the *Carteggio* a challenging read, but nevertheless it is the first detailed record ever made of many important old-master instruments.

Cozio did not always show the same respect for the old masters as we do today. We wouldn't dream of meddling with a Stradivarius, but Cozio saw Stradivari's work as part of an on-going journey towards perfection, and had no qualms about writing his own notes in ink all over his moulds, thinning out the backs of his violins if he thought them too thick, altering the angle of their necks to give them the power they needed to play a contemporary repertoire, and fitting longer fingerboards and new bridges in place of the originals. He commissioned Pietro and Domenico Mantegazza to do this work for him in Milan. At that time most luthiers put all their energy into making new violins, but the Mantegazza brothers were the first to offer a repair and restoration service. They also acted as Cozio's consultants, helping him confirm the provenance and authenticity of new acquisitions to his collection.

When Napoleon invaded Lombardy in 1796, Cozio took the precaution of moving the violin collection from his home in Casale Monferrato to Milan, where he stored the instruments in the cellar of the house of his old friend Carlo Carli. The French occupation was a time of great turmoil for most of the population of Lombardy, but not Cozio. He was a true dealer by now, and he grasped the opportunity to find new French customers. However, as I sorted through my late mother's possessions, it was not Cozio's life as a dealer or connoisseur that interested me, but his role as a biographer to all the Cremonese violins he handled over the years, preserving and promoting their life stories almost as much as the instruments themselves. If anyone in the trade had something to teach me, it was him, for now it dawned on me that when it came to my mother's things, it was their stories that really mattered most. That's the thing about things.

Tarisio

The Beginning of an International Trade in Cremona Violins

Cozio had laid the foundations for a trade that would eventually make Cremona violins an international commodity and carry them all over the world. And yet as he grew older his passion seemed to wane, and by his mid-seventies it was family history that really interested him, ousting violins from their old place at the front of his mind. By now another dealer was preparing to succeed Cozio as the most knowledgeable violin dealer and connoisseur in Europe. His name was Luigi Tarisio, and like Cozio, he was born in Piedmont. But there the similarities ended. Cozio's father had owned a castle, but Tarisio was the son of a peasant farmer. Cozio had no need to earn a living, while Tarisio began his career as an itinerant carpenter, tramping all over Piedmont in search of furniture to restore. When he reached a town or village he would settle down in the piazza to busk on his violin, which was his way of advertising to people who might have furniture that needed mending.

Tarisio's work took him to monasteries, churches and private houses, where people who had heard him play in the piazza would often show him their old violins as well as their broken furniture. Many of those instruments came from the workshops of old masters, but they had been lying about, unloved and forgotten, for generations. With his craftsman's eye Tarisio saw through the damage and dust and recognized exquisite workmanship wherever he saw it. He examined every violin he encountered with the attention of a doctor examining a patient, and committed its details to his photographic memory. In this way he developed a connoisseur's instinct for the work of old-master luthiers. Unlike Cozio, who made written notes about every instrument he saw, Tarisio never recorded any of his discoveries because he was virtually illiterate.

Nobody knows exactly how Tarisio could afford to buy his first violins, but it is often said he had a sly system for acquiring the forgotten instruments he found among cobwebs in attics and back rooms. Money was never part of his strategy. Instead he would offer to take a violin away and mend it, and then, as if it were an afterthought, he would suggest a swap between that squeaky, battered old Stradivari, Guarneri or Amati and the new instrument he had acquired for next to nothing and just happened to have in his bag. People often fell for this ruse, and so Tarisio gradually built up his own collection of valuable violins.

When he was poking about in the dusty corners of back rooms, sheds and attics at the beginning of his career, Tarisio often discovered old-master violins with their original labels. This taught him to recognize a genuine label when he saw one, although he felt no need to share the privilege for he is often accused of being the first to meddle with the signatures on violins. Sometimes he would alter the date on a label, and sometimes swap one label for another, so that an Andrea Guarneri would become a Guarneri del Gesù, or the date on an early Stradivarius would topple over the threshold of his 'golden period'. In this way, Tarisio laid foundations for the shadowy and uncertain practices that haunt the violin trade to this day.

When I first began to think about Lev's violin, I imagined that following its story would take me ever deeper into Italian history, but Tarisio changed all that when he packed six old Cremona violins into a sack in 1827, slung it over his shoulder and strode off towards Paris. At that moment the history of Italian violins turned into a truly international story, its ink spreading like a stain all over the developed world. I might have turned away at this point, for it had been Italy that first drew me to Lev's violin. And yet when I thought of it being somewhere among that exodus of instruments, carrying its own cargo of stories, curiosity drove me on. At first I imagined this cargo amounting to no more than tales from its own life, and the lives of the people who had played it. Then I realized that, like every other old Italian violin , it also carried a much larger, violin-shaped story about Italy's social and cultural life. In the story it shared with all its ancestors and cousins, Lev's violin inspired the first sonatas and concertos, changed the experience of going to church for ever, fed its voice into the diplomacy and display of courts all over Italy, and revolutionized performance by spawning the first orchestras. And when I looked back at the way Lev's violin had lodged itself in my mind, I realized it had revolutionized my life as well by propelling me towards a completely new experience of music. Thinking about all the things I had done since hearing it for the first time, I began to feel as if I were the subject of some bizarre experiment. What would happen to a woman willing to hold on to a story year after year, warming it between her hands and allowing it to unfold in any way it liked? What would happen to her life if she remained utterly suggestible and gave it the authority to teach her, delight and disappoint her in any way it chose? I was in the process finding out, and so now I turned my attention back to Tarisio slogging across the Alps. He already knew exactly what he was going to do when he got to Paris, and so he went straight to the Rue de Bussy, where Jean-François Aldric – one of the great names in French violin-making – had his workshop. As Tarisio walked through the door, Aldric took one look at the holes in his boots and the dust on his clothes, and greeted him with the disdain that only a man who had lived in Paris for forty years could muster. And as Tarisio's French was too poor to bargain with, Aldric forced him to accept very low prices for the treasures he pulled from his sack.*

This experience taught Tarisio everything he needed to know about working in Paris. On his next visit he stepped out of a carriage, elegantly dressed. He had already arranged appointments with all the leading violin dealers, including the legendary luthier, dealer and connoisseur Jean-Baptiste Vuillaume. This time Tarisio played his cards right and managed to trigger a bidding war for his stock.

* Toby Faber, *Stradivarius: Five Violins, One Cello and a Genius*, Macmillan, 2004, p. 112.

Meanwhile in Italy, where even the residents of Cremona seemed to have forgotten the golden age of violin-making, old-master instruments now had little value. Take them over the Alps to northern Europe, however, and their prices seemed to rise with the altitude. Tarisio was the first to recognize this phenomenon, and soon he was working with leading dealers in London as well as Paris. Nobody knew what to make of him in London. Sometimes he dressed as if he were a rich man about town, and sometimes he appeared in drawing rooms looking as dishevelled and down at heel as the itinerant pedlar he really was. He had little education in anything but violins, but there his instinct seemed almost supernatural. He once amazed a violin collector in London by being able to name the maker and the date of all the instruments in his collection without even touching them.* This uncanny level of expertise sometimes made people uncomfortable. James Goding, a British collector, captured something of their unease when he remarked that Tarisio 'smells a fiddle as the devil smells a lost soul'.

Tarisio returned to Paris every year. And every year he told Vuillaume and all the other dealers and musicians he knew in the city the same story about a beautiful Stradivarius violin made in 1716. Apparently Cozio had managed to buy it from Paolo Stradivari in the job lot of instruments from his father's workshop. Unlike some of the other instruments Cozio bought, it had already been completed, but like them it had never been played. Tarisio had known of it for years by the time he managed to buy it from Cozio in 1823, and now he told anyone who would listen that it was too beautiful to sell again, too beautiful to play, so beautiful, in fact, that it made you want to kneel down in front of it. He refused to bring it with him to Paris, but he just couldn't stop talking about its beauty and its perfect condition. Hearing Tarisio embark on the story yet again in Vuillaume's workshop, Jean-Delphin Alard – the composer and player who was also Vuillaume's son-in-law – is supposed to have cut him short by saying 'your violin is like the Messiah, Signor

* *Ibid.*, p. 143.

Tarisio, it is always expected but it never appears.' And in this casual way the name for Stradivari's *Messiah* was coined.

In 1839 Tarisio went to Carlo Carli in Milan and asked if he could view what remained of Cozio's collection. He bought nothing on that occasion, but when Cozio died the following year Tarisio returned. Cozio had moved heaven and earth to secure the artefacts from Stradivari's workshop, and he never dreamed of parting with them. When he died he left them and what remained of his collection to his daughter, Matilda, in his will. Tarisio was now able to pay considerably less than the original asking price for thirteen violins and a cello.* Among these treasures were instruments made by Carlo Bergonzi, Giuseppe and Pietro Guarneri, Francesco Ruggieri and Guadagnini. In this way Tarisio instantly acquired some of the most prestigious instruments in Europe.

In 1855, Matilda died, leaving the artefacts from Stradivari's workshop to her cousin, Marquis Rolando Giuseppe della Valle, along with letters from Carlo Carli, and the irritable responses from Paolo Stradivari to her father's letters.

Cozio had made tentative inroads into the market for Italian violins abroad, but while he succeeded only in attracting a few French customers, Tarisio visited Paris on business at least once a year, and worked directly with the most important violin dealers in the city. And while Cozio flirted with the British market by translating his catalogue into English, Tarisio made himself an habitué of London drawing rooms. Cozio had inherited wealth, but it was violins that made Tarisio rich, and yet he chose to live like a pauper in Milan. His neighbours didn't think to look for him for several days after he died in 1854. It is said they had to batter down the door to get into his room in the tenement building where he lived, and there they found him lying on the bed with two violins clutched to his chest. The mattress beneath him was stuffed with banknotes and gold coins worth the equivalent of a million pounds today.

* John Dilworth and Carlo Chiesa, 'Luigi Tarisio, part 2', Cozio Archive, 22 November 2017.

All this took place in Milan, and yet Vuillaume was the first dealer to hear news of Tarisio's death. He knew there would be dealers all over Italy and France desperate to get their hands on Tarisio's stock, and so he wasted no time. Within an hour he had scraped together all the cash he could find and jumped on a train from Paris to Novara in Lombardy. From there he made his way straight to the little village where Tarisio was born and his sister and her family still lived. When he arrived at the farm she showed him six violins stored in an old chest. Among them was the legendary *Messiah*, and it was just as beautiful as Tarisio had told him – and anybody else who would listen. The next morning Vuillaume packed up these treasures and set off for Milan with Tarisio's two nephews. In the bleak room where Tarisio had lived and died they found violins, violas and cellos piled against the walls. Vuillaume didn't hesitate. He shook out the contents of his wallet on to Tarisio's old bed and counted his money. He had brought the equivalent of £200,000 with him. 'This is all the money I have,' he said, pushing the wad of cash and a pile of coins across the blankets towards the two boys.

Vuillaume returned to Paris with the *Messiah*, five other instruments from the farm and all the instruments that he had found in Tarisio's room. There were 150 of them in all, and twenty-four had been made by Stradivari.* As soon as he got back to Paris, Vuillaume set about adapting them for concert performances, not even sparing the *Messiah*. He lengthened its neck, fitted it with new pegs, a longer fingerboard and sound bar, and a carved tailpiece depicting the Nativity – a witty reference to the name by which it was known.†

Over the years Vuillaume sold off Tarisio's violins one by one at an enormous profit, but not the *Messiah*. Vuillaume's story of discovering it in that dismal farmhouse had passed into legend, so that it was now the most famous violin in the world. He could have sold it for any price he liked to name, and yet he could not bear to part

---

* Faber, *Stradivarius*, pp. 143–5.

† Jon Whiteley, *Stringed Instruments*, Ashmolean Museum, Oxford University Press, 2008, p. 56.

with it. He kept it in a glass case in his house on Rue Demours aux Ternes, where it seemed to compel him to copy it again and again.*

After Vuillaume's death in 1875 the *Messiah* passed to his son-in-law, Delphin Alard, the man who had given the violin its name in the first place. Its next move came in 1890, when it was bought by Alfred Hill in London. He could only raise the £2,000 he needed by coming to an agreement with a wealthy Scotsman called Robert Crawford, who bought it on Hill's behalf, promising to offer it back to him at a fair price.† It had still been played by only a handful of people when it entered the Hill Collection in 1904, and its varnish was still as fresh as it had been when Stradivari hung it up to dry.‡

The *Messiah* appeared so new that it almost seemed to bring Stradivari back to life, and yet in Cremona lutherie had been all but forgotten by the time Tarisio died. The *botteghe* that lined the narrow streets of Isola were gone, and in 1869 San Domenico, the massive church containing Stradivari's tomb, was demolished, and the square surrounding it was turned into a public garden and renamed Piazza Roma. Nobody thought to preserve Stradivari's remains, and by the time Hugh Haweis arrived in the 1870s everybody in town seemed to have forgotten all about him. Haweis was a London clergyman, violin player and writer, and he came to Cremona on a kind of pilgrimage, much as I had done. Building up to the account of this visit in his book, he explains that he told himself he would 'go and see where the great Stradivarius lived for ninety-three years, and loved and laboured with such steadfast earnestness and such wondrous cunning, that for 180 years hardly a capital of the civilized world has ceased to do homage to his power . . .' But of course this was not the case in Cremona, and when Haweis arrived

* *Ibid.*, p. 147.
† Faber, *Stradivarius*, p. 170.
‡ Charles Beare, 'The Life of a Masterpiece', in *The Absolute Stradivari: The 'Messie' Violin 1716/2016*, Catalogue for 'Lo Stradivari Messia torna a Cremona' Exhibition, 2016, pp. 26–7.

at the railway station and asked to be driven to the *casa* – or house – of Stradivari, the cabby replied, 'What *casa*? . . . I do not know the name.'*

The only Stradivari anyone in Cremona seemed to know was a local solicitor. Haweis got so frustrated that he eventually made a very un-English exhibition of himself, standing up in his carriage in Piazza Roma and shouting at passers-by to demand if any of them knew where Stradivari had lived. A few stopped, but only long enough to say things like 'I think that the person you mean who made violins is dead . . .'

* H. R. Haweis, *My Musical Life*, Longmans, 1868, p. 317.

Third Movement

Old Italians

Violin Dealing for a Modern Age

I have always liked old Italians. When I was younger the phrase meant only one thing: the old men I saw sauntering along the streets of Italian cities, propping up the bar with an espresso in one hand and a newspaper in the other, or buying peaches in the market. Compared with the old people I knew at home, these men were like birds of paradise. They flung red scarves around their necks, wore trousers as bright as semi-precious stones, and met my eye with a look that seemed to forget the fifty-year gap between our ages. I never took up any of those unspoken invitations, but I did go out with an older man for a time. At least he seemed old to me, being in his mid-thirties. He devoted himself to rubbing down the Anglo-Saxon corners of my character and trying to remake my personality into something more Mediterranean. Of course there were some things he could never change, as even he must have realized as he looked down at my pale body sprawled under the sun on a Sicilian beach, and issued another of his stern instructions. 'Go brown now,' he said, 'not red.'

But how things do change. When I think of old Italians now, I think only of antique violins, because that is what they are called in the violin trade. Lev's violin was supposed to be an 'Old Italian' from Cremona. Its owner had told me he valued it more than any instrument he had ever owned, and yet a dealer told him it was worthless. With this contradiction always at the back of my mind, I was particularly struck by a story told to me by Connie, our youngest daughter. It had nothing to do with violins, and yet it seemed a perfect illustration of all the different ways the same object can be valued by different people. A friend had been staying with her for the weekend. On Saturday morning this friend announced she was going shopping. Nothing unusual about that, except that she left the house with no wallet and only a lollipop in her bag. Connie was careful to explain that what happened next was not entirely her friend's idea. It was her version of an experiment inspired by Kyle MacDonald, the American famous for managing to exchange a red paperclip for a house in a series of online trades.* Nevertheless, it must have been her idea to make a lolly the starting point for her own experiment in barter, and I appreciated the pun.

A twenty-two-year-old can never value a lollipop in quite the same way as a child, and so it was lucky for Connie's friend that a couple of little boys had set up a stall in the street outside the house. And it was even luckier that one of them was perfectly happy to swap a plastic model of a character from *Star Wars* for her edible version of cash. With this new currency in her bag, the friend's next stop was a clothes shop that happened to belong to a model collector. This was lucky too, and luckier still, the only figure he needed to complete his *Star Wars* collection was the very rare one she had acquired so casually on the street. The little plastic model had taken on disproportionate value in his eyes, so he didn't think twice before inviting the girl to swap it for anything she wanted in his shop. As it happened, she wanted a brand-new pair of leather trousers. And she got them.

Cash is a more likely currency for acquiring a violin, and yet there are surprising parallels between Connie's story and the forces at work in the twenty-first-century violin trade. Just like that plastic model of a character from *Star Wars*, an Old Italian can become a collectors' item, and part of its value will always be its scarcity. Take Stradivari's instruments; he made over a thousand of them during his long career. This was a considerable achievement, but wars, accidents and other calamities have taken their toll over the centuries, and only half survive. And when it comes to Guarneri del Gesù's violins, the situation is even more precarious. He made fewer

* oneredpaperclip.blogspot.com

instruments – just 250 in all – and of these a mere 150 are left. From the moment Cozio laid the foundations for an international violin market, the demand for these violins and all the other Old Italians was always going to outstrip supply. However, violins are also the tools that musicians use to make their livings, and so their evaluation of an instrument will always focus more on its technical abilities and the quality of its voice than its provenance. I understood this now, and yet I was still as indignant as ever at the thought of someone in the trade declaring Lev's violin worthless. Driven by an impulse to understand the market that could make this brutal judgement, I got in touch with Florian Leonhard, one of the world's most respected dealers in and restorers of Old Italians, and a great authority on instrument values.

I arrived at Leonhard's London office at dusk one autumn evening. It looked much like any other lovely house in Hampstead from the outside, and inside the front room was more drawing room than office. I sat down on a large sofa to wait for Leonhard, noticing just in time the Yorkshire terrier sleeping deeply on a tapestry cushion at one end. Listening to its tiny snores, I tried to gather my thoughts. I had been following the trade in Old Italians from its beginning, and this visit would bring the story up to date. But there was something else. Ever since I first heard about Lev's violin, I had been trying to find out more about church instruments. You see, initially I accepted everything I was told, and if you had known as little about violins as I did then, you would probably have done the same. But it didn't seem to matter how long I hung around in the music sections of libraries, in luthiers' workshops or Alpine forests, I could never uncover any more information about church violins, or the tax loophole that the violin player had described with such care. If anyone can tell me more it will be Leonhard, I told myself, because he had been immersed in the history of Old Italians for over thirty years.

There was a television crew in the house that day and Leonhard had to extract himself from filming to come and talk to me. Cutting a dapper figure in his suit, he took me up to a room on the first floor, where gleaming brown necks protruded from a dozen narrow wooden stalls along one wall. I knew that among them would be some of the finest instruments in the world, because Leonhard is one of very few dealers who handle violins worth upwards of $1 million on a regular basis. We began our conversation about value here, at the top of the house and the top of the market, where Leonhard explained that the thoroughbreds in the stalls were valued almost as much as investment opportunities as musical instruments. Most investments are affected by world politics and financial crises, but those Old Italians could weather any kind of tumult, and continue to increase in value year on year. We didn't talk figures, but in an article published by *Newsweek* in 2014, Leonhard is reported to have said that the past decade saw the price of an average Stradivarius increase by 10.9 per cent, with some instruments increasing in value by up to 20 per cent. Jonathan Moulds, a banker, violin player and renowned collector, owns several Stradivarius, Guarneri del Gesù and other Old Italians that he lends to star players. In the same *Newsweek* article Moulds is quoted as saying that his collection tripled in value over fifteen years.* It was no surprise then when Leonhard told me that this sector of the market attracts hedge-fund managers, banks and the foundations set up by wealthy individuals or syndicates drawn to this unusually secure way to diversify their portfolios. Although an instrument at this level will always be valued by some for its musical performance, an investor may value it even more for its performance in the financial market. This means that instead of being compared by musicians to other violins, these elite instruments are compared to stocks and shares, property, art, antiques and other 'collectibles' and 'investment opportunities'.

Many of Leonhard's clients at the top of the market have philanthropic as well as financial motives. They plan to lend their violin to

* Elisabeth Braw, 'Stradivariuses, the Latest Financial Fiddle: Investors are Using Stradivariuses as a Hedge Fund', in *Newsweek*, 22 May 2014. https://bit.ly/2kxFzPt

a prominent musician as soon as they buy it, and often go shopping with a particular musician in mind. Any investor generous enough to loan out their instrument will reap rewards, because an Old Italian's value increases with every virtuoso performance. And by translating money into objects so dense with cultural meaning, these investors also enhance their own reputations, making themselves the focus for a new kind of social recognition.*

When I spoke to the owner of Lev's violin, he told me he had been lucky enough to borrow it for years before he bought it, but many successful musicians are not fortunate enough to receive a violin on loan. They form another sector of the market, where the violin reverts to its true identity as a tool, valued for technical qualities and abilities. However, Leonhard described the relationship between the value systems of investors and musicians as fairly fluid, because of course musicians also appreciate beautiful violins with long and illustrious histories, and investors must find technically brilliant instruments if they want to loan them to top players.

A good musician has a unique sound, as unmistakable as a singer's voice. It doesn't matter what instrument she plays, her sound is always there. And yet everyone knows that the right violin can enhance that sound, which makes choosing a violin an anxious and emotional process. Leonhard compared the job of helping a musician choose between different violins to helping someone in a quandary over potential marriage partners. He knows exactly what musicians value about an instrument, but in true therapeutic fashion he never tells his clients what they need, preferring to let them discover it themselves. However, he does encourage them to play a repertoire that will allow a violin to really show off what it can do. 'And in the end,' he says, 'everybody needs the same things, vibration, colours, response and power.' These are the qualities that a musician values, qualities that Lev's violin has given its owner in such abundance.

* Fred R. Myers (ed.), *The Empire of Things: Regimes of Value and Material Culture*, School of American Research Press, 2001, p. 12.

Every violin in the room had been through a thorough investigation, because this was where Leonhard issued certificates of authenticity to Old Italians and all the other fine instruments he handles. Anyone can issue one of these certificates, but few have the expertise or track record to be trusted, and Leonhard is one of this elite. He can draw on his thirty-five years of experience, his photographic archive, and his own photographic memory to identify a violin, and yet he told me that it can still take several days to reach a conclusion through what he described as a process of elimination. Hearing this, it did make me wonder how long that dealer had taken to examine Lev's violin and calculate its zero worth.

Like Cozio or Tarisio, Florian Leonhard is that mysterious thing, a connoisseur. All three developed an instinct for the provenance of violins by handling thousands of different instruments over many years, and each had a photographic memory. Cozio backed up his observations with copious notes, and no doubt Leonhard does the same. However, he can also photograph every violin he handles, producing the sort of detailed images of its body that you might expect to find in a medical textbook. Once these technical photographs are done, the violin strikes a dignified pose on a green velvet chair at the far end of the room. Pictures taken here are not mug shots or passport photos, for the elegant chair is surrounded by studio lights that can be used to create the nuanced atmosphere of a formal portrait. Cozio's and Tarisio's expertise was built on instruments they had handled, but modern dealers like Leonhard have another advantage because they can also refer to the images of Old Italians shared on the internet by thousands of other luthiers from all over the world.

Florian Leonhard enjoys worldwide respect, but the violin market is esoteric and largely unregulated, and for this reason it has always attracted criminals. Tarisio never balked at altering a label if it would improve the value of one of his instruments, and experts in Cremona told me that people still stop at nothing to give violins false Cremonese provenances. Fortunately experts like Leonhard can usually spot a label made from paper that hasn't aged as it should, one signed unconvincingly or with ink that has faded in the wrong way, or been printed using technology of the wrong period. Other criminals commit more complicated crimes. Among the most scandalous of these crooks was Dietmar Machold. For many years he was a supremely influential violin dealer, renowned for his expertise in the seventeenth- and eighteenth-century Italian instruments that he supplied to world-class orchestras and lent to star musicians. In 2011, however, a very different story emerged when he took out a loan from a German bank for €5.9 million, setting two Stradivarius violins against the sum as security. The directors of the bank were uneasy about the loan, and so they called in a dendrochronologist to run tests on the violins Machold had left in the vault.

Dendrochronology – the science of tree-ring dating – is most often used to date the wood in old buildings or the panels of old paintings, but when applied to the rings in the Alpine spruce of a violin's belly, it can reveal when and sometimes even where the tree it was made from grew. The tests on Machold's violins revealed that the two trees had been felled long after Stradivari's death, so that instruments valued at almost €3 million apiece were actually worth only €2,000 each. It turned out that Old Italians had long been Machold's tools in a complex strategy that allowed him to pass off fakes and manipulate prices. He would even tell clients that he was making every effort to sell their violins for them, when he was actually using them as security against bank loans even larger than the one that led to his downfall. No wonder Leonhard always provides a dendrochronology report with his certificates of authenticity, because, as he puts it, they give the client scientific proof to back up his conclusions.

By now I felt I was more or less up to date with the history of this nefarious trade, and I understood that dealers and investors would always use very different systems for valuing violins. However, I had one more thing to ask Florian Leonhard, and it was a killer question:

'Have you heard of church violins, Mr Leonhard?'

His response was so carefully phrased and so full of double negatives that it took some unravelling. He hadn't not heard of church violins because they didn't exist, which they probably did, but neither had he seen a single example of one in over thirty years of handling and researching Old Italians. 'Perhaps this is something you could tell me about?' he said graciously. If only I could.

Out on the street it was dark and there was a stiff wind blowing, and as I walked towards the Underground station I began to feel a fool. I had expected Leonhard to be able to tell me all about church violins, but now I knew he had never heard of them I began to wonder if they existed at all. And if they didn't, what else might be untrue about the story of Lev's violin?

Little Italys

The Diaspora of Italians and Their Violins

The next morning I decided I must track down the musician who owned Lev's violin, and find out who told him that it was a church instrument. I had never taken his contact details, and months had gone by since we last bumped into each other at that summer festival in Wales. Luckily it wasn't difficult to find him on the internet. His name was Greg, and although I had only seen him play Klezmer on Lev's violin, I learned that he had a parallel existence as a classical musician with a full-time position in one of Britain's best-known symphony orchestras.

It was easy enough to dash off an email asking if we might meet, but what happened next reminded me of a time when Connie was very young and she put a message in a bottle and threw it in the river. Eight years passed before she got a letter from a man who had found the bottle washed up on the riverbank several miles downstream. 'You will be surprised to hear from me,' he wrote. And so she was, especially as he signed himself Neptune. Like Connie, I cast my message to Greg into a limbo of eddies and cross- currents, and then waited a very long time for his reply. From now on this would be the routine whenever I wanted to get in touch, because if he was not deep in rehearsals with the orchestra, he would be shut into a recording studio, and if he wasn't playing at a festival on a remote Scottish island, he would be holed up in an isolated cottage frantically working towards the deadline for a new composition. I soon taught myself to forget all about the message I had cast into the unknown, just as Connie had done. And in the end we always did manage to get in touch, and then Greg could not have been more kind, helpful or loquacious.

On this occasion we met in the middle of Glasgow and went for a coffee. 'My grandfather was a storyteller,' Greg said, apropos of nothing in particular. He looked out of the window of the cafe. 'If he'd seen those dogs out there' – I looked down on to the street, where a small spaniel was making friends with a husky – 'he would have come home and said there was a man with a wolf, a real wolf on a lead in the middle of Glasgow.' Now the dogs were touching noses and wagging their tails. 'And by the end of the story the wolf would have eaten the other dog, in front of all those people.' I wondered for a moment what impact this inventive gene might have on his answer, but nevertheless I asked my killer question. How did Greg know that his violin was a church instrument? His answer took us back to a time when he was still borrowing the violin from Lev. He had already been playing it for years, and now he decided to formalize their relationship by making it his own. Of course, they both needed to know how much it was worth before he could do that, and so Greg took it to be valued by a Cremona-trained violin-maker, dealer and auction-house expert, with a good reputation and a lifetime's experience. There's no doubt Greg inherited the gift of storytelling, because I lived every moment of what happened when he handed over the instrument and watched the dealer spin it between his hands, giving its old body only a cursory glance over the top of his thick glasses before pronouncing it worthless. Greg was probably hoping for a modest valuation, but I could tell his feelings had been hurt, and mine were hurt too. 'How can it be worthless,' he had said, 'when it has such a beautiful voice?' When Greg told me what happened next, he mimicked the dealer's voice for my benefit. He is a good mimic and so I understood that the high-shouldered shrug he performed as the dealer's only response to his question must have employed every one of the old man's New York genes. Then he turned away from Greg, stretched out his arms as if to embrace the empty room, and muttered 'He says it's got a beautiful voice?' Instead of answering, Greg grabbed Lev's violin and began to burn out the most beautiful tune he could think of, as if this could change the man's mind. As the music finished the dealer turned to address his imaginary audience again. 'Yes, it's got a beautiful voice,' he said, 'but it's still absolutely worthless.' And as if to leaven this crippling judgement, he went on to say that it came from Cremona, adding that it was a church violin, and explaining how it would have come to be made. We don't always believe dealers in any trade when they are trying to sell us something, but he wasn't trying to sell Lev's violin. Quite the reverse. It wasn't his to sell, and anyway he said it was worn out, and advised against buying it in the strongest possible terms, so that Greg had every reason to believe him.

I asked Greg what else he knew about his violin's past life. He told me it had lived in Russia with Lev, the Jewish musician who had lent and then sold it to him. The transition from Catholic Italy in the eighteenth century to Soviet Russia in the twentieth could scarcely have been greater, and yet Greg skipped over this great ravine in its life without comment. Afterwards I looked at a map, and marvelled at the distance Lev's violin had covered, crossing mountains and mighty rivers and plumbing Russia's deep south, where Lev said he bought it in about 1980 from an old Roma violin player in Rostov-on-Don, twenty miles inland from the Azov Sea, and not far from the Ukrainian border. I knew enough about the violin trade by now to realize that the instrument could have made this journey in a series of sales and purchases, moving slowly and inexorably east from Cremona towards Russia as it blessed one player after another with its beautiful voice. However, violin music was as much an Italian export as the violins that played it, and while it was taking the Italian peninsula by storm, music was also sweeping over Italy's borders into the rest of Europe, so that by the end of the seventeenth century, Italian players were roaming the continent with their violins and their Italian repertoire as if it were their back garden. Greg had done nothing to reassure me about his version of the violin's early life as a church instrument, for he was simply passing on a story, just as I have done. However, there was one thing I now knew for sure, Lev's violin had been in Russia by 1980. But how did it get there? That was the question on my mind when I started prying into the lives of the Italian migrants who picked up their violins and played their way across eighteenth-century Europe.

There was a hierarchy of violins and violin players on the move at that time. At the top of it were the Old Italians who made stately progress with their virtuoso players between London, Madrid, Vienna and the most prestigious Germanic courts, Prague, Paris and St Petersburg. They did not just deliver Italian music, they performed it in ways that amazed audiences everywhere. Charles Burney was never easy to impress, but he declared himself 'really astonished' by the performance of the virtuoso Giovanni Piantanida in 1770. Judging by his account, passion was still the defining feature of an Italian virtuoso performance, just as it had been when Corelli shocked audiences all over seventeenth-century Europe. Apparently Piantanida displayed 'all the fire of youth, with good tone and modern taste', despite being 'upwards of sixty years of age'.*

When virtuosi went on tour they often set out to make money and go home as soon as possible. However, almost every court in Europe had its own orchestra in the early eighteenth century, and there were plenty of other Italian violinists willing to take permanent jobs abroad in those rich and powerful settings. Of course native musicians could easily have played all the Italian music printed in foreign editions and circulated everywhere, but that wasn't good enough for some patrons. They wanted real Italians in their households, with real Italian operas, oratorios, cantatas and sonatas bred in the bone, and they hired them from the other side of Europe with the same insouciance as they hired chefs, painters or mercenary soldiers. The job of finding and selecting the right players could be tedious, and so patrons would often delegate it to their ambassador in Italy. If he was too busy or too grand, they asked his secretary, found an agent, or contacted one of the Italian

---

* Charles Burney, *The Present State of Music in France and Italy*, Elibron Classics, 2005, p. 124.

impresarios who roamed Europe in search of just these kinds of opportunities.*

The lower levels of the musical hierarchy were crammed with anonymous violin players who left Italy in search of work. They generally had no jobs to go to, but nevertheless they set off across the border full of optimism, for they knew that Italians and their music were welcome everywhere. Nothing rivalled the popularity of opera both at home and abroad, so many violin players joined travelling opera troupes. The sound of Italian music was soon so familiar everywhere that some people even attribute the beginning of a sense of cultural cohesion in Europe to the influence of those musical migrants from Italy.† In 1774 there were so many musicians of every sort abroad that one contemporary observer remarked, 'There is no corner of Europe so remote that you will not find there a few Italian singers and players . . .'‡ He could easily have included Russia in this statement, because that path was already well trodden. In 1730 a comic opera troupe is said to have travelled to Moscow via Warsaw. How did that go? Fine, according to the *prima donna*, who didn't even mention the huge detour they had to make around the marshes and wolf-infested forests near Kiev, adding six weeks to their journey, but complained only of a shortage of chocolate.§

Violins and their owners regularly made similar journeys, and four years later the Neapolitan violinist Pietro Mira and the composer and violinist Luigi Madonis went from Italy to St Petersburg to work at the court of Empress Anna Ivanovna. Almost as soon as he arrived, the Empress sent Mira all the way home again with

* R. Strom (ed.), *The Eighteenth-Century Diaspora of Music and Musicians*, Brepols, 2001.

† Gesa Zur Nieden, in *Musicians' Mobilities and Music Migrations, Biographical Patterns and Cultural Exchanges* by Gesa Zur Nieden and Berthold Over (eds.), Transcript verlag, Blelefeld, 2016, p. 9.

‡ John Rosselli, *Music and Musicians in Nineteenth-Century Italy*, Batsford, 1991, p. 17.

§ *Ibid.*

instructions to hire the best opera troupe money could buy, along with a company of comic actors and an orchestra. He trudged in again a year later having made the 2,600-kilometre journey from Venice yet again, but this time in the company of over thirty outstanding Italian violin players and other musicians, singers and dancers, actors, set designers and technicians, including the Neapolitan composer Francesco Araja, whom Empress Anna appointed her *maestro di cappella*. In this role Araja saturated Russia's imperial court with Italian music, satisfying the Empress's demand for a new opera on every state occasion, a new *intermezzo* in her court theatre every Friday, ballets on request and spectacular entertainments for her birthday and the anniversary of her coronation. Empress Anna was so pleased by Mira's work as her impresario that in 1736 she gave him the title of court jester. This may sound like a back-handed compliment, but it was said to be a more prestigious title than that of composer or violin player. Mira stayed in St Petersburg for nine years, while Luigi Madonis worked as solo violinist for the Russian court for over thirty years. The sonatas for violin and bass that Madonis composed and dedicated to the Empress in 1738 were some of the first musical scores ever printed in Russia.*

It didn't matter whether Italian violin players went to work in Russia, France or Austria, for they created a little Italy wherever they went, performing only Italian music, living together and eating, talking and playing only with each other. One of these communities flourished in Prague between 1724 and 1734, but Prague's little Italy was different because it was a colony of Venice's operatic world. Among those violin players and *prime donne*, set designers and librettists, gossip was of nothing but music and musicians in Venice, and for ten years they came and went between the two cities as if that 750-kilometre journey were a pleasant stroll. If the eastward journey of Lev's violin had begun in this way, I imagine it would have set off from Venice as part of a crowd, for as well as singers, violinists and other musicians there was the composer to

* Marina Ritzarev, *Eighteenth-Century Russian Music*, Ashgate, 2006, pp. 39–41.

set the texts, the music copyist, set designer and costume maker. They had all been auditioned or interviewed by Antonio Denzio, a tenor and old pro with plenty of experience in the theatres of northern Italy. He was acting on the instructions of a Venetian impresario called Antonio Maria Peruzzi, who had permission to stage the first operas ever seen in Prague.*

There were also babies, children, husbands and wives among the crowd, as well as the mothers or sisters of all the unmarried women. Lev's violin would have been loaded with all the musical instruments and other possessions on to carts, where children perched on top of pre-painted theatre flats, and babies were bedded down among costumes and bales of fabric. Their route took them from Venice to Verona, and then through the Brenner Pass. In just over two weeks they arrived in Linz, where Denzio received a letter from Peruzzi. He had realized, rather late, that the aristocracy left Prague *en masse* in summer, emptying the city of potential opera-goers. Prague is already over 750 kilometres from Venice, but now Peruzzi asked them to extend their journey by a hundred miles or so to north-east Bohemia, where Count Franz Anton von Sporck was waiting for them on his country estate.

No doubt they were tired by the time they reached Count von Sporck's enormous house, and it wouldn't have taken them long to realize that although most people in eighteenth-century Europe were crazy about Italian opera, Count von Sporck was not one of them. All he had wanted from them was a performance to impress a visiting princess with an influential husband at court in Vienna. She had already left by the time the troupe trailed in, dusty, dishevelled and unlikely to impress anyone. And yet securing the services of a Venetian opera troupe was a social coup anywhere in eighteenth-century Europe, so that von Sporck happily made do

* Much of my information about Peruzzi and his troupe comes from Daniel E. Freeman, 'The Opera Theater of Count Franz Anton von Sporck in Prague', in *Janacek and Czech Music: Studies in Czech Music, Volume 1*, M. Beckerman and G. Bauer (eds.), Pendragon Press, 1995.

with impressing his neighbours and visitors from Prague and Silesia by allowing everyone to assume he had brought the company from Italy at his own expense.

If Lev's violin had been part of Peruzzi's troupe, it would have spent the rest of the summer performing opera three times a week to cosmopolitan audiences in holiday mood, as well as providing table music at von Sporck's banquets and waltzes at his summer balls. At the end of the summer the troupe went to Prague at last, where the company lurched on for a decade. Peruzzi was the moneyman with no money, the manager with no organizational skills, and he was ever present in Prague. He and Denzio were locked into a punitive contract, a financial arrangement that Peruzzi had devised but could never fulfil. He would not pay Denzio as he should, they fought over who should direct each production and which new texts the composer should set. Peruzzi fell out with Count von Sporck and was accused of speaking offensively to a local magistrate. Denzio eventually managed to wrestle control of the company into his own hands, but the finances were already deteriorating. Von Sporck wouldn't help and Denzio's career ended in a debtors' prison, a story still told to dampen the spirits of any Italian impresario hoping to make a commercial success of opera.

When a company failed in this way – as they sometimes did all over Europe – violin players and their instruments moved on. But wherever they went Italian violins spoke just as clearly as they had at home, because Italian music was a universal language. Some violins would eventually be brought home again like faithful servants, but others must have been sold abroad, broken and abandoned, stolen or given up to pay off debts, so there was soon a diaspora of Italian violins almost as large as that of musicians. Perhaps Lev's violin was part of this breadcrumb trail laid by musical migrants all the way to Russia.

Despite the failure of individual impresarios and their troupes, the popularity of opera grew and grew, so that by the early nineteenth century a composer like Rossini could expect to be treated as a superstar anywhere in Europe. Or as Stendhal put it in his biography of the composer, 'Napoleon is dead; but a new conqueror has already shown himself to the world; and from Moscow to Naples, from London to Vienna, from Paris to Calcutta, his name is constantly on every tongue.' Opera found its way into Stendhal's novels, and he made La Scala in Milan the setting for a pivotal meeting in *The Charterhouse of Parma*. Neither Contessa Pietranera nor Count Mosca care much about which opera is on stage, because they are too busy looking at each other across the auditorium, watching the theatre clock which 'warned the audience every five minutes of the approach of the hour at which it was permissible for them to visit a friend's box', and talking to each other incessantly.* I was reminded of this scene when I went to the Teatro di San Carlo in Naples a few years ago. I thought we had been lucky to get opera tickets at short notice, but it was mid-week and when we arrived there were still plenty of free seats in the vast auditorium. I wish I could tell you something about the performance, but all I remember are the old ladies in fur coats. They seemed to be everywhere, in the foyers and anterooms, in the stalls and in the gold-painted boxes that towered above us. They greeted each other across those vast spaces with cries like the calls of distant birds. Watching them, it struck me that this was just as much of a social occasion as the evening Stendhal described, and when curtain up did nothing to interrupt the flow of conversation, I convinced myself that the same sort of dramas were unfolding before my eyes in that auditorium.

It wasn't opera drawing me back to Italy now, however, but the culture surrounding it, for that was the world so many Italian violins inhabited. I might have returned to Naples or gone to some other great opera palace, like La Scala, or La Fenice in Venice, but I preferred to think of Lev's violin dominating the orchestra in the simpler and more democratic space of a small-town theatre. Rossini came from Pesaro in Le Marche on Italy's Adriatic coast, where each little seaside town had its own opera house. Standing alongside the church and the *municipio* in the central piazza, they were one of

---

* Stendhal, *The Charterhouse of Parma*, trans. C. K. Moncrieff, Everyman's Library, 1992, pp. 104–5.

the holy trinity of buildings once essential to the life of those small communities. Originally the opera house was a rough, wooden building. When it burned down – as it almost always did – the original building was often replaced by a grand structure with neo-classical pillars, fine plasterwork and a beautifully painted wooden auditorium, so that although Le Marche was one of the most isolated regions on the peninsula, it has some of the finest theatre buildings in central Italy.*

Violinists in these places depended on private investors to produce the funds for the new opera houses and theatres that would give them work. In Le Marche this capital was generally raised by consortiums of landowners looking for ways to reinvest profits from their country estates. Theatre was never an entirely reliable investment, but nevertheless these canny businessmen could expect a good return during the opera season. The rest of the money for construction was raised by selling off theatre boxes long before the building was finished. Boxes were private property that could be bought and sold, mortgaged or even rented out, just like any other property in town. The key to a box passed between generations in rich families, rather like keys to their city palaces and country villas.

When the building work was finished and a new theatre was complete, the inhabitants of Pesaro and Le Marche's other seaside towns expected a brand new opera with new sets and costumes during carnival season, on special occasions such as saints' days, and during the *fiera franca*, the tax-free business fair that attracted crowds to the town of Senigallia in Le Marche from all over Italy. This was an expensive business, but the bulk of the risk was taken by the impresario, who was expected to supply the complete package of libretto, music, performers, violinists and other musicians. In small theatres the orchestra had to be reinvented each year from a mix of local amateurs and experienced outsiders. Some of the string players would be the freelancers who toured the peninsula on a

---

* *Il Teatro nelle Marche, architettura, scenografia, spettacolo*, ed. Fabio Mariano, Nardini, 1997, p. 80.

continuous circuit encompassing the whole of north and central Italy, Naples, Catania and Palermo in Sicily.* Others would be familiar figures from the town, so you might recognize your cobbler in the orchestra, still wearing his leather apron to play the double bass.† Impresarios working in Le Marche sometimes economized still further by borrowing musicians from a military band stationed somewhere nearby, because they would play in return for no more than bed and board.‡

A passion for opera infected Italy like a disease, Stendhal even gave that disease a name. He called it *melomania*, or 'an excessive sensibility to music', and described one victim as driven by 'sheer delight' to remove his shoes during performances. This wouldn't have mattered much had he not flung them over his shoulder at the crowd when 'some really *superb* passage moved him deeply'. Then there was the notorious miser in Bologna who had overturned the habits of a lifetime by pulling all the money from his pockets and flinging it on the floor 'when the music happened to touch some supreme fibre in his being'.§ Visiting Venice in 1813, just after the triumphant opening night of Rossini's *Tancredi*, Stendhal found the whole city in the grip of *melomania*, so that he couldn't escape the sound of people performing snatches from *Tancredi*'s arias, and apparently one of the city's judges threatened to clear the public gallery at court because everybody was singing '*Mi rivedrai, ti rivedrò*'.** Some of the symptoms of *melomania* were said to be more serious, however, and there was a Neapolitan doctor who blamed Rossini for over forty cases of 'brain fever or violent nervous convulsions' among young ladies watching performances of *Mosè in Egitto*.

* *Ibid.*, p. 24.
† M. Salvarini, *Il Teatro La Fenice di Ancona, Cenni storici e cronologia dei drammi in musica e balli*, Fratelli Palombi Editori, 2001, p. 56.
‡ G. Moroni, *Teatro in musica a Senigallia*, Fratelli Palombi Editori, 2001, p. 18.
§ Stendhal, *Life of Rossini*, John Calder, 1956, p. 399.
** *Ibid.*, p. 48.

Giuseppe Tomasi di Lampedusa – author of *Il Gattopardo* (*The Leopard*) – also saw Italy's obsession with opera as an infection or even a cancer that took hold immediately after the Napoleonic wars and then spread 'with grand steps'. He believed it sucked up all Italy's energy for the arts, so that, when the mania subsided at the beginning of the twentieth century, Italy's creative life 'was like a field which locusts have ravaged for a hundred years'.*

I went in pursuit of this extraordinary phenomenon by travelling to Pesaro one October, where I arrived on a grey and windy day. I had chosen a hotel a half-hour walk from the old city centre on the promise of a sea view. A promise is a promise, and if I stood on the biscuit-sized balcony outside my room and turned my head almost impossibly sharply to the right, there it was, a sliver of the Adriatic whipped into unlikely waves by a fresh wind. By suppertime there was a sea gale blowing. It looked as if most of the restaurants on the front had already closed for winter, and the receptionist at the hotel had the sort of cold that made me want to get out of her orbit as quickly as possible. I lingered just long enough to get directions to a *trattoria* that was still open, its windows overlooking a black expanse of roaring waves. They put me on the quarantine table, the one they reserve in every restaurant for single diners. I would have liked to be among the couples at the far end of the room, but I suppose they thought I would eavesdrop, and they were right. Instead they stowed me in a corner by the sea, where the wind battered the walls and the only other table was taken by a delegation of Russian engineers.

I have never enjoyed eating alone, but like anyone who travels for work, I have found many ways to make use of a solitary meal. On that evening I took out my notebook and reread the notes I had made before leaving home. 'Rossini', I had written at the top of one page, 'born in Pesaro 1792'. He left when he was eight, but nevertheless I had already seen his genial face plastered on the sides of buses and in the windows of shops and restaurants all over town,

* Quoted by David Gilmour in *The Last Leopard*, Quartet, 1988, pp. 102–3.

and if he reminded me of anyone, it was the English writer and comedian Stephen Fry. The three-storey house where Rossini was born had been turned into a museum, there was an exhibition at Palazzo Mosca celebrating the 150th anniversary of his death, and an opera festival every summer, and the conservatoire was founded through a legacy in his will. When I looked at the menu, there he was again, for Rossini was a renowned gourmet and he is credited with inventing several rich and meaty recipes. I could have eaten a dish called tournedos Rossini if I had wanted dinner *alla francese* that night, something he must have invented after he left Italy for Paris in 1824. But although that decadent combination of tender beef fillet, *foie gras* and truffles struck me as the perfect metaphor for a sumptuous opera, it was not for me.

This was the world I had come to find in Pesaro, but the Russian engineers soon distracted me from the dogged rereading of my notes. They must have ordered with abandon, because there was barely enough room on their table for all the plates the waitress now had to deliver. They seemed surprised by every dish she brought, although she did her best to explain what they were. They had chosen to eat fish that night, and if I had been relying on her mimed impressions of a sea bass, I would have been just as confused as they were.

The next day was brilliantly sunny, but there was a cruel wind blowing in from the Balkans, a combination that my older Italian friends would describe as 'dangerous', pointing to the receptionist at my hotel as proof. I walked towards the town centre on tired sand. The hotels and bathing huts with their peeling paint were boarded up, and someone had raked all the abandoned toys into forlorn little piles. The lifeguards' red canoes were upturned, and gulls and fishermen had reclaimed the sea wall. I was on my way to Teatro Rossini, which stood, like so many of Le Marche's theatres, on the site of an older building. In this case the Teatro del Sole, as it was called, had been cobbled together in an old stable block in 1637. Apparently the auditorium had always retained its rustic atmosphere and its original beams, blackened with age. They had decorated it

with a few simple frescoes and put out some chairs for papal dele-
gates and the grander ladies in the audience, but by the beginning
of the nineteenth century local aristocrats wanted somewhere
smarter. I didn't need a map to get to the new theatre that took its
place in 1818, because all I had to do was leave the beach and walk in
a straight line down Via Rossini and through Piazza del Popolo to
the other side of town. The street was full of children on their way
to school, and there was something washed clean about Pesaro that
morning, as if it had shrugged off the grimy complications of bigger places.

Teatro Rossini was one of at least six hundred theatres that were
built or remodelled in Italy during the first half of the nineteenth
century, and over half of them were large enough to accommodate
opera productions.* Violins had been up to their necks in opera ever
since the seventeenth century, and this had always put them at the
heart of an economic phenomenon; as well as creating jobs in the
building trade, opera stimulated the economy and the circulation of
money in towns and cities all over the Italian peninsula. It attracted
tourists from home and abroad, and spawned thousands of jobs for
violin players and other musicians, opera singers, chorus members,
prompts, choreographers, dancers, set designers, costume designers, seamstresses and scene shifters.†

Teatro Rossini was a square, sandstone building, which still had
the original stable doors from the Teatro del Sole. Gargantuan and
scarred by time, they were firmly closed when I arrived, but my
appointment was with the manager, who had told me to come
round to the stage door for a lightning tour. We didn't have much
time, she explained, because the rehearsal was about to begin. She
hurried me upstairs, through a small door and into a fusty passage
lined with dressing rooms. Ushering me on, across the stage where

---

* David Gilmour, *The Pursuit of Italy: A History of a Land, Its Regions and Their
Peoples*, Allen Lane, 2011, p. 166.
† John Rosselli, *The Opera Industry in Italy from Cimarosa to Verdi*, Cambridge
University Press, 1984, p. 39.

the cast was already assembling, she jumped down with me into the auditorium. And there we were, suddenly immersed in the atmosphere of a theatre that can have changed very little since it first opened in 1818. The violinists and other musicians would have been lodged between the stage and the stalls, where a few people were lucky enough to find a bench, and the rest stood or walked about during the performance.

Four tiers of richly gilded boxes towered above us in the auditorium like the cells of a gigantic honeycomb. Those shareholders would generally have secured territory for themselves in the middle of the second tier of boxes. During the opera season, when a box became a family's private *salotto* and dining room for four or five nights a week, it would have looked as if there were a series of society portraits hanging from the walls of the auditorium, their glowing frames simultaneously enclosing and displaying the richest families in town. Prestige dwindled with every flight of stairs. Less important families sat in the third and fourth tiers, and when I climbed right to the top and emerged on the fifth floor, I found an open gallery. This was the place where the most impoverished nobles in Pesaro would have mingled with the middle classes. The audience up there was invisible, but in compensation they got some of the best views in the house.

Teatro Rossini has 760 seats, but photographs from the mid-nineteenth century show people hanging out of boxes crammed with bodies, so that there could be a thousand or more spectators at a single performance. You might expect these crowds to diminish at subsequent performances of the same opera, but not at all. The theatre was simply the only place to be during the season. The audience might arrive late or leave early as the season wore on, but they never missed a night. And while there, they might spend much of the evening talking, eating, drinking and even playing cards or sleeping, but they would break off from these activities to encore so loudly after certain arias that the singers were obliged to perform them again. Even when it looked as if no one was listening at all, great waves of emotion crossed the auditorium, and collective sighs and encouraging shouts sometimes drowned out the performance altogether.

Violins were just a cog in the vast, participative machine that was opera in nineteenth-century Italy. They worked in a fug of sweat from the performers and the crush of bodies in the stalls, and of expensive perfumes wafting out from the boxes. During the interval a cart laden with cooked tripe would be wheeled into the theatre, adding that slaughterhouse smell to the mix. In another opera house violinists might also have had to endure the stink of wee, or worse, from dark corners of corridors and remote staircases, and the smoky smell of supper being heated over small stoves tended by servants in corridors, vestibules and doorways. But Teatro Rossini was a nineteenth-century theatre, and audiences in Pesaro had nineteenth-century standards.

The same routine was repeated during the opera season in little theatres all over Le Marche. In Fano, the Teatro della Fortuna has enormous antechambers, vestibules and other public spaces outside the auditorium. This was a common feature in eighteenth- and nineteenth-century theatres, when these spaces were furnished with card tables, and theatres earned a convenient second income as casinos. Some people bought tickets that only permitted entrance to the building. They came to eat food sold in the interval and to play cards. If they changed their minds and decided to see the performance, they had to buy another ticket for the auditorium.

By the time I left Pesaro, I had spent long enough in opera houses, grand churches and illustrious courts, where Lev's violin might have played the elitist, literate, urban music known as *musica colta*. 'You've had enough of "posh violins",' one of my friends remarked, and perhaps she was right. I wanted to think about an alternative existence for Lev's violin, and soon I began to imagine it playing the *musica popolare* that once echoed through the fields and dusty villages of rural Italy, and the working-class quarters of its towns and cities.

Musica Popolare

Roma Fiddles and Italian Folk Music

Every region of Italy had its own *musica popolare*, its own sad tunes about bereavement, separation and thwarted love, and joyful ones about courtship, *carnevale* and Christmas. Music was integral to the rhythms of working life and the identities of different trades and jobs. The labourers toiling in Sicily's sulphur mines had their own music, and so did the island's tuna fishermen. The dockers at the port in Genoa sang, shepherds everywhere played their own tunes, and *contadini* – peasant farmers – had a different song for every task during the agricultural year. There were songs for sowing and reaping, picking fruit and gathering olives. Many of these jobs have been mechanized today in ways that make singing impossible, but if you happen to be in a Sicilian orange grove at harvest time, you will realize that some things never change. The pickers will throw their ladders against the trees in the morning and scramble in among their foliage. You would be lucky to glimpse even a hand or the top of a woolly hat after that, but you can always track their progress by following the sound of yet another rendition of the song they pass among the trees all day.

Music has always varied enormously from one small Italian village to the next, just like the recipe for bread, the flavour of olive oil, or the dialect spoken by the locals. There has always been such a contrast between the melodies played on the streets of Naples in the south and in the mountain villages of the north that it is hard to believe they were products of the same country. But of course Italy was never really a country in the political sense until Unification in the middle of the nineteenth century. This made travelling any distance a tedious process that involved stopping again and again at tatty customs posts to show your travel documents and have your luggage inspected by rapacious officials. And bad luck if you had already passed through an area afflicted by plague, because then you were obliged to spend a few bleak weeks in quarantine.

The difficulties that political divisions caused travellers were exacerbated by the natural contours of the landscape. The Apennines still split Italy in two by running like a spine down its centre from north to south, so that even now travelling from east to west is unexpectedly complicated. Go by train from Rome to Pesaro on the east coast, for example, and you will be obliged to travel north to Bologna, then board another train that will turn you round and take you south again down the east coast.

All this made travelling difficult, but it also helped to preserve the *cultura popolare* that was the fabric of society in every isolated community. Woven from music, songs and dances, *cultura popolare* also encompassed the instruments people played, the distinctive dialects or languages they spoke, the clothes people wore, the tools they used in fields and workshops, and the rituals and proverbs that made sense of their experiences. All of these elements varied so much from place to place that sometimes the inhabitants of neighbouring villages could barely understand each other.

Musica colta was a monoculture that seemed to rise above all these variations, for no matter what their dialect, musicians all spoke the same classical language of music. There was nothing to prove on which side of this great cultural divide Lev's violin had made its home in Italy, and it probably slipped over the boundary between *musica colta* and *musica popolare* just as it does in Britain today, playing Scottish folk music one night, and Sibelius in the Royal Albert Hall the next. I had already envisaged so many settings for its professional life playing *musica colta* that now I decided to redress the balance by setting off for the Alpine valleys on the frontier between Italy and France, where the voices of violins are still a vital ingredient in *musica popolare*. They were late arrivals in those isolated towns and villages, appearing only in the nineteenth century to join the hurdy-gurdies that had been there for centuries, playing alongside fipple flutes, Jews' harps, and the kind of bagpipes shepherds made from the skins of their sheep or goats.

Fourteen mountain valleys in Piedmont have acted like deep freezes for the Occitano language that seeped over the border from the south of France in the eleventh century, along with the music and poetry of the Troubadours. Despite being suppressed, ignored and superseded over the centuries, Occitano has survived so successfully that approximately half the population of the valleys still speak one of its numerous dialects, and Occitan music is so popular that more than sixty bands in Italy are dedicated to playing it.

The inhabitants of Occitania have never had a country to call their own, and yet you can get there easily enough by jumping on a bus outside the station in Cuneo and heading north-west towards Valle Maira. It was autumn when I made this journey, and the foothills of the Alps were softened by a fuzz of trees with leaves the colour of violin varnish. Alternating swathes of mown and unmown maize lined the road, a ragged patchwork of yellow and faded green. With each village we approached, maize gave way to apple orchards, hazelnut groves and small industrial estates that had been dropped into this patchwork as if they were just another kind of produce. One of them had a forecourt full of green cranes, a flock of machines penned up like gigantic farmyard birds. I jumped off the bus in Dronero – or Draonier as it is in Occitano – at the head of the Maira Valley. It is old fashioned and unselfconscious, and it has the look of a place that knows something about snow. Arcades line the main street, making dark caverns of little shops stocking cardigans for old ladies, chestnut-roasting pans, penknives, axes and down jackets sold by their weight in grams. The River Maira goes crashing through the bottom of the town, where it is spanned by Ponte Diavolo, a magnificent medieval bridge with V-shaped notches cut into the battlements that defend it.

Dronero has no need to guard itself against enemies these days, but it does have too many friends. In summer they swarm into town to walk up the mountains, and they come back again in winter to ski down them. I visited when it was in recovery between seasons, booking myself into the only hotel that was still open. On my way there I paused to read posters advertising films, concerts and excursions into the mountains, but all the dates were long gone, as if they had given up on entertainment in Dronero at the end of September. After checking in, I asked the hotel manager for a map of the town. He told me he had long since run out, and why would he restock when the only thing he felt like saying to tourists was 'Get lost'?

The hotel was full of dark rooms, dark furniture and dark paintings. 'Take your key with you if you go out,' the manager said, 'because I am going home now, and without it you will be locked out.' The key was ancient and enormous, and it had worn a wide hole around the lock in the eighteenth-century door to my room. The window overlooked a little piazza and a building draped in just the right amount of Russian vine. Its leaves had already turned red, and there was snow on the mountains all around us, but that didn't matter to me because I was not reliant on the seasons like other tourists. My mission was to visit Rosella Pellerino, the scientific director of Espaci Occitan, the Occitan cultural centre, library and museum on the edge of town. Rosella grew up speaking Italian at school, Occitan with her mother's family and Piedmontese dialect with her father's. No wonder she chose to be a philologist. She is steeped in the music, language and culture of these valleys, and has plenty of friends among violinists who play *musica d'òc*, and the musicologists who have collected and studied it over the years.

What happened next was a story in two parts. The first part was Rosella's to tell, and she sat me down in the library at Espaci Occitan and told me all about the life that gave rise to the music she loves. When she described Dronero in the nineteenth century it sounded like the sort of place where, despite hard work and harsh conditions, everybody knew how to party. They could all play an instrument, dance and sing, and she said they were always swapping places, so that one day's audience would be the next day's performers.

Until now I had thought of music in Italy as an export, but Rosella explained that the men and women of Dronero travelled great distances in search of work, and returned home with new tunes and dances to enrich the traditional repertoire that had accumulated in the valley like sediment over the centuries. Some of them would go to lowland cities in summer to sell their cheeses, eggs or vegetables, and the wine barrels, bowls and spoons they had carved from chestnut wood during the winter. If Lev's violin had ever lived this life, it might have spent its summers busking alongside them on a sunny piazza. Or if it had belonged to a shepherd, it would have gone up to the high summer pastures with him and his flock. Its music would have been a kind of company in that isolated place, and yet some shepherds needed more tangible companions, and so they tamed marmots to live alongside them. Rosella showed me photographs of children in Dronero with these unlikely pets draped across their shoulders, as if they thought themselves the answer to that awkward middle ground between a guinea pig and a terrier.

People returning from these relatively local journeys might have brought back a few new tunes, but it was the ones who went further afield that made the difference. Some of them mended umbrellas or sharpened knives on the piazzas of big cities in northern Italy, some got jobs washing up in London or Paris, and others went to pick lavender or harvest olives in Provence. There were always violin players and other musicians among these migrant workers, and some of their names are still famous in the valleys. Giovanni Conte – or Briga as he was known – would set off on foot for France and Spain each winter, sometimes staying away from home for years on end. He was a one-man band, and he sang songs from the valleys while playing the hurdy-gurdy, beating the drum on his shoulder with a stick that he moved with a string tied to his ankle, and shaking the bells on his hat to keep time.

Everything Rosella said about *musica d'òc* in her valley would have been a distant memory if not for Gianpiero Boschero, whom she had invited to come to the museum that afternoon and tell me about his work. It was a long story, and he tackled it with such brisk competence that it was no surprise to hear he had only recently retired from his career as a lawyer in Saluzzo. His story started in the 1970s, when he began spending summers in San Maurizio di Frassino, a village high in the Val Varaita. 'I was 20 that first summer,' he said, 'and I was studying law. There were lots of kids of about my age or younger in the village, as well as the children of émigré families from Provence or Paris.' Everybody wanted to dance on those long summer nights, but Boschero and his friends soon got bored, because the sole musician in the village was an old bloke who could only play a couple of tunes on the mouth organ, which meant they had to perform the same dances again and again. Soon they began to ask older people in the village to teach them traditional Occitan dances. 'I could ask a neighbour to run me through a particular sequence of steps at any time of day or night,' he recalls, 'and then I would go on and on practising until I got it right.' He realized that the dances, music and songs he was learning must be recorded if they were to survive after the older people in the village were gone, and between 1971 and 1975 he dedicated Sunday each week to going from house to house in San Maurizio and other villages to record music, songs and dances. 'Because I spoke Occitano,' he recalls, 'every door was open to me. Even though they didn't know me, I was one of the family.' He was no ethnomusicologist, but he says he applied the same scientific rigour to the task of preserving music on his cassette recorder as he did to studying law at university. As time went on, he began to take batches of recordings to a friend who knew how to transcribe them. Despite his lack of musical training, Boschero found that he could pick out any wrong notes in the transcription because, as he put it, 'I had the music inside me.'

Over the years Boschero collected about twenty-four dances and numerous local variations. 'And as I learned them,' he says, 'I taught them to my friends, to keep them alive and stop them becoming museum pieces.' Seeing Boschero and his friends dancing each summer amazed other young people in the villages, who had always been ashamed of the valley's old traditions in front of outsiders. Now they began to join in with the dancing, so that

Boschero's project gradually revitalized the culture of music and dancing in the valley in ways that he could never have imagined. 'We weren't like a dance troupe,' he said, 'trying to revive something and wearing special clothes to do it. We just danced as we were, because this was no performance, and the first to learn dances in this way were not even great dancers. But those that followed were better because they got their grandparents to teach them. Now they are in their forties and they are teaching their own children, and the tradition carries on. These days lots of children are learning hurdy-gurdy and accordion, there are many local luthiers and dance teachers who give Occitano dance classes in schools from Genoa to Turin.'

Boschero made a number of recordings of Juzep da' Rous, the greatest Occitano violin player in the valleys. What he told me about Rous's violin was disappointing because it made it seem much less likely that Lev's violin had ever been an Occitan instrument. Like so many other people from those Piedmontese valleys, Rous and his wife had spent years working in Paris. While he was there, Rous bought the violin he played until the end of his life, asking his wife to look after it when he died, or at least, he said rather poignantly, to stop the grandchildren 'dragging it around the house on a string, like a dog'. Boschero had seen plenty of violins in the valleys over the years, and he said that most of them were French. So much for my vision of Lev's violin in that romantic Alpine setting. Rosella even explained that the paths down the mountainside into France were much easier than those into Italy, so that it was natural for Occitan violinists to look to France for their instruments.

Rous was a traditionalist. He went on playing until he was well into his eighties, preserving the songs and dances of the nineteenth century. Since his death in 1980, Boschero's work has inspired young violinists and other musicians to approach traditional music in a different way, and there has been such an explosion of interest that you can find huge crowds dancing to *musica d'òc* in Genoa, Turin and even Milan on almost any night of the week, and at festivals in the mountains during the summer. And if you had dropped into Espaci

Occitan that afternoon, you would have seen Boschero and Rosella dancing solemnly around the library.

Lev bought his violin in Russia from an old Roma musician, and so now I made finding out about Roma music in Italy part of my strange pilgrimage in pursuit of the tired old story I had inherited from Greg and carried with me for so long. I began by visiting Santino Spinelli. He is a Roma academic and author, a tireless campaigner for the rights of his community and, above all, an accordion player. This makes him a busy man and he never replied to my emails. His wife sent me a kind message, though, and a list of all the gigs lined up for her husband's band Alexian Group, some in Italy and some abroad. There was only one date I could manage, and it meant I would see Spinelli play on his home patch in Abruzzo, the region that acts as lynchpin between Italy's fat waist and its slim legs.

The train carried me slowly down the east coast on the line Mussolini built to link Bologna to the Mezzogiorno. If Fascist engineers had felt any sympathy for swimmers or sunbathers they would have blasted a railway tunnel from the mountainside, but they didn't and so we travelled within touching distance of shelters made on the beach from bleached sticks, abandoned at the end of summer like remnants of some former civilization. Inland, it was autumn. The sunflowers were over, heads drooping, and flights of birds cartwheeled above ploughed fields.

Now I am going to tell you all about what happened when I got to Abruzzo, because if I paper over the gaps, there will be nothing left to tell. I had prepared for our meeting by reading one of Spinelli's books. It told me there have been Roma – or *Rom* as they are called in Italy – living in Abruzzo for so long that their presence is imprinted on the urban landscape. In the old quarter of Ripateatina near Chieti, for example, you can walk down Via dello Zingaro, or Gypsy Street, up Salita dello Zingaro, Gypsy Hill, and into Largo dello Zingaro, Gypsy Place.* Like other long-established communities in

---

* Santino Spinelli, *Rom, Genti Libere, storia, arte e cultura di un popolo misconosciuto*, Dalai editore, p. 76.

central and southern Italy, the first Rom in Abruzzo were probably fleeing the Ottoman invasion of their old home in the Byzantine Empire. They would have travelled over what is now former Yugoslavia, settling briefly in the Habsburg Empire before crossing the border into Friuli Venezia Giulia and travelling south to Abruzzo.* The language of *Rom abruzzesi* still bears the imprint of their journey across Europe in words derived from German and Serbo-Croat.† They also nurture their own musical repertoire, and there are subtle differences between the songs and dances of every Rom community in Italy. Like Roma music everywhere, however, theirs incorporated the fluid melodies and complex rhythms that would blur boundaries between *musica colta* and *musica popolare* by inspiring composers such as Rossini, Verdi and Donizetti.‡

I left the train in Pescara, hired a car and headed south towards Lanciano, a pretty town straddling such a steep hill that I drove up the streets in first gear and down them with my eyes half shut. Lanciano's usual claim to fame is a miracle involving a sceptical eighth-century monk whose faith was reignited when he saw bread and wine transformed into real flesh and blood during the Eucharist. These days something more substantial – as opposed to transubstantial – is happening there. It is Santino Spinelli's home town, and his efforts combined with those of an enlightened town council have made it one of the only places in Italy where Rom feel welcome. Or, as someone later explained to me, 'there is a sweet wind blowing through Lanciano, and we can only hope that one day it will begin to blow through the rest of Italy.'

The following morning I drove up the *autostrada* again to attend a conference devoted to the forgotten genocide of Roma and Sinti during the Second World War.§ The main lecture theatre of the

* *Ibid.*, p. 82.
† *Ibid.*
‡ *Ibid.*, p. 268.
§ Sinti refers to members of the minority living in western and central Europe, and Roma to those in eastern and southern Europe.

university in Chieti was already packed with students from local secondary schools, and Alexian Group was scheduled to open the proceedings. I sat at the back with the naughty students, the chatterers who came and went while their teachers kept their backs firmly turned. But even they were gripped when Spinelli's band began to play. It was only ten in the morning, and yet from the first note to the last the music was in full flood, whipping up passion with a mix of joy and longing, manic energy, exuberance and grief. Santino was centre stage, pushing the music towards climax on the accordion, while his son made heart-stopping swoops and slides on the violin, and his daughters beat out the rhythm on double bass and harp. 'Hep, hep, hep,' Santino yelled, and soon we were all clapping in time and some of the kids were dancing in the aisles.

The music finished too soon, and we settled in for a gruelling morning of lectures on the war's forgotten tragedy, the story we prefer not to tell about up to a million Roma and Sinti exterminated by Nazi and Fascist forces. The Roma call this *Samudaripen*, which translates literally as 'everybody dead'. This genocide has never been acknowledged by the Italian government, and there has been only one memorial erected in the whole of Europe to those who died, although that was about to change.

It was over, and I ran down to the front of the hall to speak to Spinelli. I wasn't the first to have that idea, but when I eventually reached up to the stage to grasp his hand I said, 'Santino, it's me, I've come from Britain to talk to you!' Had I known the scale of the events he was involved in organizing, I would never have chosen that week for my visit, but he grabbed my hand and said, 'Let's eat together in Lanciano tonight.' 'Where?' I said, and as the crowd began to part us again, he called out 'Teatro Fenaroli'.

Teatro Fenaroli is a thick-set nineteenth-century theatre squashed into a side street off Lanciano's Piazza Plebescito. I should have seen it coming, but nevertheless I was surprised to find a buffet for two hundred people laid out in the neighbouring building. You could always tell where Santino was by the flash of his white jacket through the crowd gathered around him, and I was sure they had very much more pressing things to discuss than the history of Rom violin music in Italy. I prodded at a miniature lasagne from the buffet with a tiny wooden fork, sipped prosecco, and talked with anyone who would. But these were people with grief on their minds, people brought together by the memory of events that had left great spaces in their histories where family should be, and this made any questions I might have about music seem too trivial to utter. I sat for a while with a couple of the speakers from the conference, solemn, erudite Roma men, and told them why I had come. 'You are an academic,' I said to one of them – and indeed he was. He had spoken that morning about his research into the medical atrocities inflicted on Rom children by the Nazis. 'I am planning to write something about Rom violin music,' I told him, 'what advice can you give me?' 'Just be very, very careful,' he replied, 'remember that it sometimes takes me three months to write a single sentence, and that if you get anything wrong, it will be there for ever.' 'No pressure then,' I might have said, but didn't.

After dinner we all went into the theatre next door for the prize-giving of the Amico Rom (Gypsy Friend) Arts Competition. Spinelli has been organizing this event for twenty-five years, selecting a committee of judges to award prizes to artists, writers, actors, musicians and film directors in Roma and Sinti communities all over Europe. Prizes are also awarded to anyone in the *Gage* (non-Roma) community who has shown dedication to defending their rights or championing their culture. Santino was master of ceremonies that night, and he selected a different celebrity from the international Roma community to award every prize. When it came to giving a prize to the First Violin in the local symphony orchestra he called on Orhan Galjus, founder of a pan-European Roma radio station broadcasting out of Amsterdam. I had chatted to Galjus earlier, and now I saw him hop nimbly on to the stage and stride across it with the trophy in his hand. When he reached the violin player he said, 'Let's swap. I'll give you your prize and you give me your violin.' Santino was delighted. 'Oh Orhan!' he bellowed into the microphone, 'How wonderful, are you going to play for us?' Galjus took the violin and bow from their bewildered owner, lifted his hand as if to play and turned to face the audience. Afterwards I wondered whether he had been scanning the rows of seats for my face when he said 'Just because I am Rom, it doesn't mean I play violin.' I will never know if he was speaking to me, but I heard him all the same.

Writing about violins in conjunction with Rom music will always be a cliché, but nevertheless they found their way into Rom music just as they did into every other musical tradition on the Italian peninsula. Spinelli is a great historian of music and songs, and in his book *Rom, genti libere*, he describes the music passed across generations from the old to the young as a means of building and maintaining the sense of identity in a family or community. That is where the real music is, according to Santino, in the family, where it is 'an expression of the soul' and a means of preserving and passing on memories, traditions and feelings.*

The grand finale came the following morning, when I joined a small crowd gathered in a park on the edge of Lanciano to witness the unveiling of a memorial to all the Roma and Sinti people in Europe lost to genocide during the Second World War. The town band played and then we stood in drizzle to have our hearts wrung again by a series of speakers from all over the world. When the moment came to unveil the statue of a Roma woman clasping a child, her long skirt caught on barbed wire, I had to look away from the depth of sorrow on faces all around me.

I said I would tell you everything about my journey in pursuit of Rom music, and so I will. Back on the train in Pescara I headed north towards Florence, where I had arranged to meet Sister Julia Bolton Holloway. I have known Sister Julia ever since I interviewed her for an article about her unusual job as custodian of the Protestant cemetery in Florence. She is not paid for the work she does there, and so she lives on her modest pension. Or part of it, because she uses the rest to pay members of the Rom community to work for her in the cemetery

---

* Santino Spinelli, *Rom, Genti Libere, storia, arte e cultura di un popolo misconosciuto*, Dalai editore, pp. 259–60.

as stonemasons, metalworkers and gardeners, traditional skills that have been nurtured by their families over generations. She also pays the women in the community to come to literacy classes at the cemetery, so they can teach their own children to read and write. If anybody could introduce me to a Rom musician, I thought, it was Sister Julia.

I have known Florence ever since I lived there as a teenager. Its water still smells so old and dark that even turning on a tap reminds me of the thrill of being far from home in that beautiful place for the first time. When I met Sister Julia she explained at once that the Rom families she knew were craftsmen, not musicians. That's the way it was, trying to find out about Rom music in Italy, nothing turned out as I hoped. I remember there were always musicians playing on the steps of the Duomo when I lived there first, and I seem to remember them much more recently as well, but on that visit I couldn't find a single Rom musician on the streets.

And so instead of finding out about Rom music in Florence, I met Sister Julia's Rom friends and learned what it is like for them to live in Italy today. She took me to Mass for the homeless on Sunday morning. There were rucksacks piled at the back of the church, and a promise of breakfast after the service. We sat near the front and the pews behind us soon filled up with homeless men and a scattering of Rom women wearing long skirts. After a sermon about love it was time for communion. 'Why are none of the Rom going up to the altar?' I whispered to Julia. 'Because some people in the Diocese don't believe in giving communion to Rom,' she replied, rather loudly I thought. I have loved Florence for years, but on that visit, I saw its underbelly and felt I had never really known it at all.

Fourth Movement

Twice Looted

The Fate of Old Italians during the Second World War

We have a friend who loves old cars. Not vintage ones, not sports cars, just old, broken cars. He devotes weekends to fiddling about in their engines, mending their torn upholstery and restoring their bodywork until they gleam and purr again. I couldn't stop trying to find ways to make the life story of Lev's violin run more smoothly, and as time passed I began to wonder if I wasn't a bit like him. I had already plastered over the hole at the heart of its story with various kinds of migrant musicians, and now I felt I had to consider the darker possibility that Lev's violin had moved across Europe to Russia with many thousands of other instruments looted during the Second World War. Following this route was bound to take me to some of the war's ugliest and most depraved chapters, and the idea of dipping into all that pain and suffering on such a flimsy pretext made me so uncomfortable that I spent a couple of days convinced I should abandon the idea. And yet the path was there, and it led directly to the real and verifiable history of Lev's violin in Russia.

When you think of the Second World War, violins are not the first thing that springs to mind, and yet once I began to look I found them everywhere. Sometimes they were among the swag of looting armies, sometimes among the forlorn heaps of possessions piled on the railway stations of concentration camps. And it was not only physical violins I found, for both their voices and their music were embedded in the history of Nazi Germany and the war. Their cultural importance was apparent as soon as Hitler became Chancellor in 1933. Almost at once he passed a law forbidding Jews from taking jobs in the public sector, so that Jewish musicians were sacked from the state-funded orchestras of cities, theatres and opera houses. This wreaked havoc on the string sections of orchestras all over Germany because, as everybody already knew, a disproportionate number of their players were Jewish. Now the Nazi Party turned its attention to the music those denuded orchestras performed, removing the works of Jewish composers – past and present – from concert programmes and radio broadcasts. This turned out to be another way of silencing the voices of violins, because among the works orchestras were now forbidden to perform were violin concertos by Mendelssohn or Schoenberg. In the obsessive and distorted world built around anti-Semitism, even Handel and Mozart had to be reassessed. Handel had used texts from the Old Testament for his oratorios, and this could only be put right by turning *Judas Maccabeus* into *William of Nassau*, while *Israel in Egypt* became *Mongol Fury*. The problem with Mozart was his collaboration with Jewish librettist Lorenzo da Ponte on *Così fan tutte*, *Le nozze di Figaro* and *Don Giovanni*. This could be resolved by performing the operas in German, although it was unfortunate for the Nazis that the most popular translations had already been made at the end of the nineteenth century by the conductor Hermann Levi.*

As anti-Semitism was propagated and normalized, the looting of Jewish property in Germany and Austria became endemic. Some Jewish families suffered casual thefts by opportunistic neighbours or passers-by, and others were the target of the government-sanctioned looting carried out by a task force within the Gestapo code-named Möbel-Aktion, 'Furniture Action'. It was set up in 1938 to empty the homes of Jewish families that had fled, been deported, imprisoned or murdered. This was robbery of a grubby and intimate kind. Violins were plundered alongside the great communities of objects that settle around families over the years, the china and children's toys, jewellery, saucepans, paintings and ornaments that remind each generation of both the greatest and most banal events in their family histories; of the geography of their migrations and settlings;

* Erik Levi, 'The Aryanization of Music in Nazi Germany', *The Musical Times*, vol. 131, no. 1763 (January 1990), pp. 19–23.

of their fortunes, good and bad, their aspirations, enthusiasms, tastes and beliefs. A violin found among these families' possessions might have been played at bar mitzvahs, family weddings and funerals for generations, so that it had become a vessel overflowing with memories. Torn out of context, it shed all meaning.

Violins and all the other possessions looted by Möbel-Aktion were sorted, repaired and repacked in depots set up by the Nazis in the centre of Paris. This strange, sad work was done by Jewish workers from an internment camp in one of the city suburbs. Thousands of crates arrived every day for them to sort, and it's said they sometimes found half-written letters, and even plates with the food still on them.*

Möbel-Aktion picked anonymous violins out from among the furniture and sold them off to raise money for the war effort, or passed them on to Aryan students whose own violins had been destroyed by Allied bombing. Meanwhile, Old Italians and other fine violins were being looted for a quite different purpose. After a trip to Italy and the museums of Florence, Rome and Naples in 1938, Hitler had conceived the idea of a new Führermuseum in the Austrian city of Linz, where the *crème de la crème* of antique violins would be exhibited alongside looted masterpieces of every kind from all over Europe. The museum was key to Hitler's megalomaniac vision of his old home town as the new cultural centre of Germany. There was also to be a new university, an opera house, and a conservatoire. And as if all that was not enough, Linz was to have a symphony orchestra to rival those of Berlin and Vienna, a national radio orchestra, and an annual music festival honouring Bruckner, just as Bayreuth honoured Wagner.†

Old Italians were targeted by a special force called Sonderstab Musik, set up in 1940 to amass the world-class collection of instruments that Hitler dreamed of seeing in his Führermuseum. It was

* Robert K. Wittman and David Kinney, *The Devil's Diary: Alfred Rosenberg and the Stolen Secrets of the Third Reich*, William Collins, 2016, p. 362.
† Erik Levi, *Music in the Third Reich*, Macmillan, 1994, pp. 212–13.

staffed by an erudite team of musicologists, scholars and instrument specialists, shameless experts who followed in the wake of the Nazi invasion of France, Holland and Belgium, accumulating fine antique violins among other valuable instruments, original music scores, books and recordings. Every violin stolen in this way was identified, assessed and meticulously recorded before being packed into a crate and loaded on to a freight train for Berlin. Only one of those careful inventories survived the war. It is a nine-page, typewritten list of stolen instruments that was stored in occupied Paris. Among the gems were an Amati, two Stradivarius violins and a Guarneri del Gesù.*

By 1942 almost 70,000 Jewish households in France, Holland and Belgium had been pulled apart and robbed of tangible objects and the invisible culture that surrounded them. The combined income from sales of stolen goods and money confiscated from Jewish businesses and bank accounts amounted to nearly 120 billion Reichsmarks – over £12 billion at the time – enough to fund a third of the Nazi war effort.

The Nazis had stripped Jewish violinists of their instruments and their jobs, they had silenced violin music by Jewish composers past and present, and yet violins were made integral to daily life in the concentration camps where so many Jews were interned. Between 1939 and 1943 over a hundred concentration camps were built in Italy and occupied territories. The majority held prisoners of war and political opponents, but many became deportation camps for Jewish, Roma and gay prisoners who were later transferred to extermination camps north of the Alps.

Music is often credited with having helped some people to survive in concentration camps, but Szymon Laks, a Polish violin player who became conductor of the camp orchestra in Auschwitz II, seems to have been determined to demolish the romantic idea 'that music kept up the spirits of the emaciated prisoners and gave them the strength to

---

* Howard Reich and William Gaines, 'How Nazis Targeted the World's Finest Violins', in *Chicago Tribune*, 19 August 2001.

survive'.* In his words, 'Music kept up the "spirit" (or rather the body) of only the musicians, who did not have to go out to hard labour, and could eat a little better.'† Nevertheless, he attributed his own survival to a series of miracles, all involving music. First he was accepted into the camp orchestra, despite the fact that he had forgotten the ban on Jewish composers and chose a Mendelssohn violin concerto as his audition piece. Then he was promoted to the role of music copyist and chief arranger for the Birkenau Men's Camp Orchestra, a role that saw him transcribing marches from memory and composing new ones in the German style. He never explains what instrument he found to play, but SS officials are known to have confiscated violins for the orchestra from the area around Auschwitz.‡

Laks also described the 'sea of people' arriving in cattle trucks at Auschwitz station, where they were forced to abandon everything they brought with them on the platform. There would certainly have been violins among those 'heaps of valises, suitcases, bags, parcels and bundles filled with food, tidbits, alcohol, jewels, money, gold coins, and various kinds of precious objects – all of which the owners would never see again'. Jacques Stroumsa, an amateur player from Greece, wrote about bringing his violin with him when he was deported in 1943. He held on to his pregnant wife with one hand and his violin with the other when the train arrived at Birkenau, but was forced to let go of both.§

By whatever means they were acquired, Laks was dazzled by the selection of brass and woodwind instruments hanging on the wall in the orchestra barracks, and the piles of violin cases lying on a purpose-built shelf. With a violin in his arms, he found that he could look at the electric wires surrounding the camp for the first time without being tempted to end his life by running at them.

* Szymon Laks, *Music of Another World*, Northwestern University Press, Illinois, 1989, p. 5.
† *Ibid*, p. 117.
‡ James A. Grymes, *Violins of Hope*, Harper Perennial, 2014, p. 116.
§ *Ibid*, pp. 111–12.

The camp orchestra was made up of gifted amateurs and of professional musicians from military bands and orchestras. They played marches every morning as the prisoners left the camp for forced labour, and again when they staggered back, sometimes carrying or dragging the corpses of those who had died of exhaustion, hunger or illness. As the camps grew, it could take two hours of ceaseless music to accompany the workers as they marched in and out, morning and evening. The orchestra was also under orders to play outdoor concerts of light music every Sunday afternoon, and to create a cheerful facade for visits from Nazi luminaries or the International Red Cross.

Henry Meyer was another violin player in the Birkenau Men's Camp Orchestra. He had been a child prodigy, and SS officers in the camp soon chose him to play at their parties. 'What did we play for them?' he wrote. 'American melodies. Americans were their biggest enemies. Who were the composers? Gershwin and Irving Berlin: Jews. Who played? Jews. And who listened and sang along with these schmaltzy songs until tears rolled down their faces? The members of the SS, our tormentors. What a grotesque situation.'* Laks also commented on the extraordinary impact of his music on their oppressors. 'When an SS man listened to music,' he said, 'he somehow became strangely similar to a human being. His voice lost its typical harshness, he suddenly acquired an easy manner, and one could talk with him almost as one equal to another.'†

The rightful ownership of Italian violins in Europe had already been overturned, but now there was another great shuffling of the pack, because Germany invaded Russia in June 1941, and Nazi troops behaved with such brutality that from 1943 the Soviet government began planning to strip Germany of all kinds of property in compensation for its ruined palaces and churches, ransacked villages, and denuded galleries and libraries. Reparations for these terrible losses were to be claimed by the Red Army and a series of trophy

* *Ibid.*, p. 134, quoting Henry Meyer.
† Quoted by James A. Grymes, *Violins of Hope*, Harper Perennial, 2014, p. 134.

148

brigades staffed by teams of experts in every aspect of the arts. What happened next has been described as 'the most prodigious secret removal of looted cultural property in human history'.*

The Arts Committee in Moscow chose art historians, connoisseurs, instrument experts, museum curators, picture restorers and artists as members of the trophy brigades. The objects of 'cultural value' they were ordered to seek out included musical instruments. The Soviet government wanted to conceal this secret operation from the Allies, and so although the members of the trophy brigades were civilians, they were all issued with the uniforms of officers in the Red Army.

The brigades followed in the wake of the Red Army, and this could be very problematic because Soviet troops killed, plundered and destroyed everything in their path. 'We are taking revenge for all of it,' one of them wrote in a letter home, 'and our revenge is just. Fire for fire, blood for blood, death for death.' All ranks were involved in unrestrained, personal looting, so that commandants were too busy 'collecting watches, typewriters, bicycles, carpets, pianos . . .' to pay proper attention to protecting the possessions of large country estates, theatres and museums. Everybody had their own enthusiasms, and violins, being infinitely portable and full of the promise of hidden value, were a perennial target.

The brigades found Italian violins in museum collections, in the houses of German citizens, and among caches of objects seized by the Nazis in France, Belgium and the Netherlands, or confiscated from Jews bound for the concentration camps. The Trophy Brigade of the First Ukrainian Front thought they had stumbled on violin gold when they happened upon four battered violin cases in a military commandant's office in Silesia. The violins were stored among a stash of pianos, bicycles, sewing machines and radios, and when they removed them from their cases, they found one labelled as a Stradivarius of 1757, and another signed by Amati with an illegible date. They can't have noticed that the first violin was dated twenty

* Akinsha Kozlov, *Stolen Treasure*, Weidenfeld, 1995, p. xvi.

years after Stradivari's death, because they immediately removed it to a secure location. Later they found several more 'Stradivarius' and 'Amati' instruments, and realized that none were genuine.

In a sense, violins dragged backwards and forwards between Russia and Germany were no different from all the other objects plundered from museums and houses during the Second World War. They were just more things among furniture, blankets, wrist watches, pianos and children's toys stolen from Jewish families, or prosthetic limbs, women's hair, money and gold teeth stolen from the living and dead in concentration camps. And yet violins were often so much more than that. Their voices had been the sound of celebration in the Jewish shtetls of Eastern Europe and ghettos everywhere, of street music played by travelling Jewish musicians all over Europe, of music written by famous Jewish composers, and of the famous Jewish musicians who played it. By stealing violins the Nazis had taken another step towards achieving their ultimate goal of erasing every trace of Jewish culture. Was Lev's violin caught up in this ugly process? I would never know, but pursuing yet another version of its life story had taken me to places in war-torn Europe I would never have been.

Full Circle

Revival in Cremona

While Cremona violins were being shuttled across Europe, something radical was happening in their home city. It seemed to have forgotten all about the violins at the heart of its history for at least two hundred years, but just before the outbreak of the Second World War there was the beginning of a slow revival, first of interest in the history of lutherie tradition, and then in lutherie itself. If you want to see the catalyst for this slow revolution, you must go to Cremona's Museo del Violino in Piazza Marconi. Walk through the gallery with its glittering display of fabulous instruments and into a room lined with plan chests, their shallow drawers half open. The tools displayed there won't look like much until you realize that the tiny finger planes, chisels, knives, callipers and scrapers were Stradivari's, their wooden handles still greasy with sweat from his own hands, and their blades worn thin from sharpening. Commonplace and practical, old and worn as they are, their mere presence in Cremona triggered a process that would haul the city back to the heart of global violin-making.

Despite becoming a very successful dealer in violins and all the artefacts associated with them, it never crossed Cozio's mind to sell those precious relics. After his death in 1840, they passed first to his daughter and then to his great-nephew. You might think his great-nephew's wife a philistine for finally putting them on the market in 1920, but it turned out to be the best thing she could possibly have done.

Marchesa Paola della Valle was on the point of selling the relics to the French ambassador in Rome when she received a letter from Giuseppe Fiorini, one of the most important luthiers in Europe. Like Cozio, Fiorini recognized the power of objects to inspire us in ways that can alter the course of our lives, and he realized the potential of Stradivari's relics to help him realize his dream of opening a violin-making school where all the old Italian techniques could be taught. 'I took a quick decision,' Fiorini told a friend, 'and wrote to Marchesa Paola Della Valle something like this: "I am not a rich man and I am not a profiteer wanting to conclude a deal; on the contrary, I am a luthier and a scholar, willing to buy the Stradivari relics and use them in order to improve the art and ultimately to give them to the Italian Government, if it will be willing to open a school of lutherie. Please do help me, Madam, to reach that patriotic goal."' That done, he drained his life savings, took out an additional loan, and secured the collection for the equivalent of £37,000.*

Fiorini offered the tools and other relics to several cities with the proviso that they set up a new Scuola Internazionale di Liuteria, dedicated to teaching violin-making at the highest level, appoint him its principal, and put Stradivari's tools on public display. Cremona was the first city to accept his offer. The relics were handed over in 1924, and the search began for premises to house the new school.

The bicentenary of Stradivari's death was in 1937, but the school was still not ready to open. Nevertheless Roberto Farinacci, Fascist mayor of Cremona, could not let the occasion pass unmarked, for he recognized the bicentenary's potential as a focus for propaganda about Italy's glorious past, and the golden age of violin-making in particular. He went straight to the top with his plans and won personal approval from Mussolini – a violin player himself – for two exhibitions. *L'Esposizione Internazionale di Liuteria Antica Cremonese* was to be a magnificent display of Old Italians from Cremona, and *La Mostra Nazionale di Liuteria Moderna* would showcase the work of 119 contemporary luthiers from all over the country. All of their instruments were automatically entered in a competition for which the government made 70,000 lira (£25,000) available in prize money.†

* Toby Faber, *Stradivarius: Five Violins, One Cello and a Genius*, Macmillan, 2004, p. 200.
† *Ibid*, p. 201.

When it came to finding Old Italians to exhibit, the organizers had a problem because, ever since Tarisio turned them into an international commodity at the end of the eighteenth century, they had been travelling further and further from home. By putting out an international appeal they eventually managed to amass thirty-nine violins, violas and cellos and a harp, well over half of them from America.* Farinacci, who would soon be promoted to Secretary of the Fascist Party, prepared Cremona for an influx of visitors from home and abroad by remodelling the city centre. Perversely, this involved demolishing the buildings on Piazza San Domenico where Stradivari and Guarneri had once lived and worked and made many of the violins that would be displayed in the exhibition, and bulldozing the rest of Isola and replacing that intricate web of streets and workshops with a grid of straight roads and buildings designed to express the modern-minded power of the Fascist government. Among these new buildings was Palazzo del Arte, the handsome structure that now houses the Museo del Violino, and the relics that triggered both a renewed interest in lutherie and these bizarre actions ensuing from it. The bicentenary celebrations were a triumph. They only lasted for a month, and yet more than 100,000 visitors poured in from all over the world to see the exhibitions and attend concerts staged to coincide with them.†

Farinacci had made sure there was nothing left of Isola, but that didn't stop me from pedalling over there when I was last in town. I leaned my bike against the bandstand, wandered along senseless, curving paths in the public gardens laid out on the site of the old church of San Domenico, and looked around me for any trace of the crafts that once thrived on Isola's narrow streets. But the only artisan products I could see were the craft beers fuelling noisy conversations between students at a bar overlooking the gardens, where pigeons were enjoying their own *aperitivo* of crisps and focaccia crumbs under the tables. Despite the loss of Isola and all that it

* *Ibid*, p. 201.
† Faber, *Stradivarius*, p. 201.

represented, the Scuola Internazionale di Liuteria opened in 1938, and the dreams of Count Cozio and Giuseppe Fiorini were realized at last. Tragically it came too late for Fiorini, who had died four years earlier. Nevertheless, this would be the beginning of a new chapter in Cremona's history, a chapter that would eventually bring it full circle, making it as famous for violin-making today as it was when Stradivari was alive. None of this could have happened without the quiet force exerted by those old tools from his workshop, for their return to Cremona had triggered an almost miraculous revival of the city's interest in its own history.

I set off the next morning to visit the school after another night in my landlady's bed. She had slept on the sofa as usual, giving up that testament to forty years of marriage and presenting me with a choice and a challenge. Which dip in the mattress to settle for, his or hers? Creeping out of the apartment that morning, I pedalled over cobbles in Piazza Sant' Agostino, past wild poppies that had seeded themselves in a bright pool at the base of the church, and emerged at the top of Via Colletta. It was already full of students, many carrying instruments in cases on their backs, so they resembled gigantic insects with ill-fitting carapaces. Everyone in the street was headed for Palazzo Raimondi, home to the Liceo Musicale, a senior school where pupils specialize in music, and one of only two state-owned lutherie schools in the world.

The first class of the day had just finished by the time I arrived, and students were surging through the courtyard at the heart of the palazzo. Some were only fourteen years old, because the lutherie school is also a *liceo,* or senior school, where they can begin to study violin-making as soon as they finish middle school. They would be at the school for five years, and by the time I met them they had already spent a first year learning how to care for tools and use them safely, how to recognize different kinds of wood, and how to predict its behaviour under different conditions.

Mixed in with those adolescent Italians in the courtyard were students of different ages from all over the world. Many had already trained in other disciplines and trades, so that during the week I met professional violin players and other musicians, cabinet-makers and carpenters, and even people who had already completed lutherie apprenticeships elsewhere. The school awards credits for relevant experience, so that some of these mature students only join the course in the second, or even the third, year and then follow a personalized curriculum focusing on the gaps in their knowledge.

I made my way through the courtyard to the violin-making *laboratorio* at its far end, where a fourth-year group was already at work. The blinds were drawn down against the blazing sun outside, and students sat in pools of light shed by lamps pulled low over benches scarred by generations of hard work. There was a library atmosphere of quiet concentration. That's not to say it was quiet, not at all. Violin-making involves the sound of scraping, cutting, gouging and planing wood, the hiss of sanding and much sharpening of tools, their blades screaming as they are pressed hard against a turning whetstone. To add to this cacophony, they were re-laying the main drain in the street outside, so we sometimes found it hard to hear each other speak.

For the Italians in the class school was free, and even the international students paid only a tiny fee each year in education tax. As well as workshops on violin-making, varnishing and restoration, they attended classes in many other subjects, including physics and chemistry, acoustics and the history of lutherie. I met most of the *maestri* that week. All of them were graduates of the school, and all had their own workshops nearby, so that they all knew about selling violins as well as making them. That morning Angelo Sperzaga was in charge, a dapper figure wearing an indigo blue scarf around his neck and a white lab coat, its breast pocket stuffed full of sharpened pencils. Looking around me, I realized that the students had developed a house style over the past four years. It seemed to work equally well for boys and girls with long hair, for they all wore tight buns on top of their heads. Over the course of the next week I would meet students from Italy, Korea, Japan, Canada, Argentina, Switzerland and France. Whatever their age or background, they were all obliged to speak Italian at school, so that some would have spent more time at language classes than lutherie lessons during their first months in Cremona. And whatever their age or nationality, they all produced violins according to the Cremona method invented by Andrea Amati 450 years before, which made me wonder if Italian violins really need to be Italian at all.

Every country has developed its own, subtly different, violin-making tradition over the centuries. I have already told you that the French use the same templates to make the back and belly of several instruments, so that one violin can be virtually identical to another. Not in Cremona. Here luthiers have always followed Amati's method of using an individual mould or form to shape the outline of each new violin, and this produces a slightly different structure every time. Clémentine, a French student, had already cut out the mould for her new instrument. Now I watched her shaping the *fasce*, six thin strips of maple that would form the ribs – or sides – around the outside of the violin's body. She soaked each one in water and then bent it to fit the hour-glass contours of the mould by holding it against a heated metal last. There's something of the kitchen about violin-making, because the ribs and every other part of the body are stuck together with glue that must be gently heated until it reaches exactly the right consistency. I soon learned not to speak to anyone engaged in the delicate processes of heating, stirring or testing. The glue's foul recipe of animal bones and skin is exactly the same today as it has always been. It isn't as strong as today's synthetic glues, but that's precisely its advantage, because the body of a violin will always move while it is being played, and if it moves too much it must be allowed to come unstuck, or it will crack under the strain. And if an instrument needs to be opened up for repair, seams stuck with this natural glue can usually be persuaded to give way without splintering or any other damage. When Clémentine had glued and clamped the ribs in place she left them to dry.

The shavings accumulating on the terracotta tiles of the floor were maple, spruce and ebony, always the main ingredients of a Cremona violin. Combine this mix with the Amati method of construction and you have the quiddity of a Cremona instrument of any age, the universal characteristics that it shares with every other violin made in the city since the mid-sixteenth century. And when it comes to wood, students find all they need in the *magazzino*, where wedges of spruce and maple are stored and indexed like a library of books on open shelves. Choosing wood is a serious business, a long sentence for the student who must work with his choice, good or bad, until the violin is complete. Felix, a friendly Romanian in his late twenties, told me that he needed to select the materials for his next project, and invited me to come down into the basement where the wood was stored. As soon as we arrived, Felix began to pull wedge after wedge of Alpine spruce off the shelves, tapping each one to test its resonance. All the spruce in the *magazzino* was cut into sections the same length as the top of a violin, then cut again into wedges that resembled the slices of an extremely tall cake. Each one was exactly half the width of a violin. When prepared in this way, spruce is said to be quarter sawn. After Felix made his choice, the quarter-sawn wedge would be split for him again on an electric saw in the *magazzino*, this time laterally into two identical pieces, half the thickness of the original. When Felix came to make the top of his new violin, he would stick the sawn edges of the wedge together, opening it out like a book.

Now Felix turned his attention to the maple that he would use to make the violin's back. *Acer pseudoplatanus* is ideal for making violins because it always retains its strength, never mind how thinly you carve it. The first violin-makers in Cremona used wood from the maples they found growing on the banks of the Po, but demand soon outstripped supply. Fortunately Venice's wood markets were always full of mountain maple from the Balkans because gondola builders in the city used it to make oars. Cross-sawing maple reveals beautiful markings, or 'figure', in the grain. Flame maple is especially popular among luthiers because its fibres grow in an undulating pattern that can look almost like flames flickering in moving light.

Felix examined the maple just as he had the spruce. This time he was looking to see if it had been cut perfectly straight along the grain when the wedge was divided in two. The two halves of a badly cut wedge might reflect the light to different degrees, he explained, and this could make one side of the violin's back look darker than the other. There was something frenzied about the way he pulled out wedge after wedge, stuffing them back on the shelves after only a fleeting glance.

'What's the matter, Felix?' I asked.

'We can't take too long or they will get annoyed.'

'They' were the men in charge down there, below street level, men with a photographic memory for all the wood in their domain. It didn't take Felix too long to select a maple wedge with a silky stripe, and then he began to rifle through a plastic box full of strips of maple to be used as *fasce*. That's when the trouble began, because those princes of the wood store knew that the ribs he had chosen were in a four-part 'set' for making a perfectly matched back, neck and scroll. And yet somehow their memories and their ledgers had let them down, and they couldn't find the other three pieces anywhere. Deep down, I think Felix suspected they didn't think him worthy of such fine wood. 'Sometimes they make students in the lower years use ugly wood,' he whispered, 'until they are skilled enough to make proper use of something better.' Nevertheless he seemed quite resigned to giving up the beautiful maple for the ribs and choosing an alternative. A man at the desk by the door checked off his final selection of wood in a ledger. He had the eyes of someone who had seen too much foolishness down there in the *magazzino*, and a blank stare that refused to register student emotion.

Maestro Sperzaga was in the *laboratorio* when we returned, keeping an eye on a student carving the arching to shape the outward swell of the belly of a violin. He was using a large gouge, and it looked like hard work. 'Not at all,' Sperzaga said, sternly adjusting the angle of his arm, 'as long as you do it like this.' And then, 'I can't understand people who want to experiment with other kinds of wood for the bellies of their violins. If you use a different wood, you can have no idea what it will be like to work. It might be so dry that it's rock hard, or it might be full of lymph.' While he was talking it struck me that he and his students were like psychoanalysts of wood, observing and taking note of its behaviour in every situation. Right on cue, Clémentine began to undo the clamps on the ribs of her nascent violin, only to find that one of the delicate lengths of maple had cracked. What happened next taught me a lot about violin-making and the school where it is taught. Clémentine picked up the mould with its damaged rib and thrust it into the hands of Maestro Ardoli, who had just returned to the *laboratorio*. He glanced at it, and then at the mute, tear-stained figure beside him, before making a very particular and perfectly judged sound. It was somewhere between laughter and sympathy, and even to me, the outsider, it seemed to say that setbacks are all part of the job for a luthier, that wood can behave unpredictably however well you know it, that we are all in it together here in the *laboratorio*, and we will help you to get back on track. And that is exactly what they did. The *botteghe* of the great masters in Isola were always teeming with skilled assistants, and it was much the same at the school, where students took a close and professional interest in each other's work, pitching in to help with gluing and clamping, or at any other moment when extra hands were needed, so that Clémentine had all the support she needed to set things right and move on.

There were instruments at every stage of their gestation in the *laboratorio*, and going from bench to bench, I chatted to the students while they worked. A boy from Rome told me he had started the course when he left middle school at the age of fourteen. Lutherie wasn't so hard, he said, and he certainly seemed to have no trouble inserting the purfling into the belly of a double bass that lay on the bench like a whale's bone, vast, pale and sculpted. Looking around me at the bellies of instruments without purfling was rather like seeing the naked face of a woman who generally wears lots of eyeliner and mascara. There is something softer and more diffuse about her face without make-up, and as I looked at those unfinished bellies I remembered that Lev's violin had much the same quality. Life had taken such a toll on its body that the purfling was never more than a fraction of a centimetre from its edges, and had even slipped off them altogether in places. Now I realized that this was the explanation for the quietness of its appearance, making it look as if it would rather not be seen.

A violin's belly is not complete without f-holes. They look like a decorative flourish, and yet they have a vital role to play, because part of the sound of a violin is created when the vibrations of the instrument's body squeeze air in and out of the f-holes. Cutting f-holes looked like one of the trickiest operations in the whole process of producing an instrument, and watching one student make a start I found myself growing anxious on his behalf. He had already traced their shapes, and now it was Maestro Negroni who stood by in his surgeon's white coat to watch him drill two very small holes in the belly, as if he were performing a biopsy. Then he inserted the narrow blade of a saw into one of these holes and started to cut the sweeping curve. Negroni never took his eyes off him as slowly, competently, the first 'f' began to emerge. 'Piano, piano,' he warned, but then more gently, 'If you break the blade, there are others.' When he had cut both holes, he refined the shapes with a knife, and then smoothed them to perfection with a file. *Che soddisfazione.*

A violin must be measured and measured again at every stage of its creation. Everybody in the *laboratorio* pulled out a metal rule and laid it across their work so often that you might begin to wonder if they all suffered from the same compulsive disorder. Luthiers were not such slaves to precision in the eighteenth century, and you only have to look at a Stradivarius or a Guarnerius to see that those old masters did not have to worry too much about their f-holes being perfectly symmetrical. Today everything is different, for as one luthier in the town told me, 'Stradivari didn't work to the millimetre, but we can't afford to make mistakes because our Japanese customers begin by getting out a ruler and checking to see that everything is precisely measured. They buy by the ruler, and if they don't find what they want in my workshop, there are 169 other *botteghe* in Cremona to choose from.'

Another student was making final adjustments to the neck of her instrument. Always with a ruler to hand, she scraped away at it with a chisel and rubbed the place smooth with sandpaper. Then she ran the ruler over it again, holding the neck up against the light to see where another fraction of a millimetre must be removed. I heard a satisfying click as she slipped the neck into place, but after more close attention to its angle, she took it out again. They are unusual people, those students, already singled out for an arcane trade that will always demand these exceptional levels of precision.

Some of the students in the *laboratorio* were also studying restoration. When I went upstairs to join one of their workshops I found myself in a very different atmosphere. Downstairs everybody focused on perfection, but in Alessandro Voltini's restoration class we were in the geriatric ward, where everyone was clever just for being alive, and there was a spirit of compromise and a cheerful determination to do the best in the face of suffering. Voltini was working on his own project, head down, light pulled low over the bench, but I interrupted him to ask if they ever ran out of violins to restore. Looking up for a moment he said 'Never, because we get lots of instruments to repair from the *liceo* downstairs. And if we did run out, all we would have to do is drop a few violins on their heads and that would give the students plenty to do.'

One of them was working on a mid-nineteenth-century violin. She told me it was German and had been brought in for repair by a woman whose uncle had played it in a concentration camp orchestra during the war. It had endlessly repeated this brutal story about its past to anybody who would look at its face, which was smashed in nasty places, and its varnish, which seemed to have absorbed all the dirt of its history. But now these brutal wounds were being treated, and soon it would begin to look like any other violin made in Germany at that time. I wondered if the family would find they valued it more or less when the bleak story written into its body had been erased.

There was a sealed door between the *laboratorio* and the dust-free environment of the workshop where Maestro Ardoli was supervising another group of students. The air in there was saturated with the smell of pine resin. Metal cages lined the far wall, and inside them violins at different stages of the varnishing process hung by their scrolls. Some were still 'in the white', entirely unvarnished, and others were different shades of golden yellow and reddish brown. Opening the cupboard full of the exotic oils, resins and colours for making varnish, I saw jars of pumice, lacquer, limonite and lycopodium, montana candelilla and carnauba waxes, and precipitations of walnut, cochineal and sandalwood – and that was just the first line in a battalion of jars and bottles.

Varnish is usually made from a combination of four things, but Ardoli encourages his students to experiment with differing proportions of those myriad ingredients to find a recipe of their own. This is the final stage in the process of making a violin. It can take as long as two weeks from start to finish, because a violin will eventually wear between twenty-five and thirty coats, and each must dry before another can be applied. Oil varnishes can be dried under a lamp, although Stradivari swore by hanging his instruments from nails in the rafters of his *seccadour* overlooking Piazza San Domenico, and drying them in the sun.

There has always been a lot of talk about the mysteries of varnish, as if discovering Stradivari's recipe could turn us all into master luthiers. His great-great-grandson claimed to have found his original recipe jotted down inside the cover of the family Bible in 1704. He made a note of it, apparently, before destroying the Bible to preserve this family secret. But Massimo Ardoli had no time for secrets, and he was ready to tell me anything I wanted to know about varnishing violins, whether with oil-based or alcohol-based varnish. 'They both have the same effect,' he said, 'it's the means of application that differs.' Whatever recipe a luthier uses, the varnish serves the same functions of protecting the wood from damp, sweat and dirt of any other kind, and from humidity, although varnish cannot stop a violin from reacting to moisture in the air, because the inside of the instrument is never sealed. Varnish also improves the vibration of the wood when the violin is played, so that the quality of the varnish does much to determine the quality of the instrument. The Hill brothers, those great experts and connoisseurs in London, went so far as to say that even a beautifully constructed violin made from fine-quality wood could be 'astonishingly bad' if it were to be poorly varnished. Ardoli compared the violin's experience of a good varnish to that of wearing comfortable clothes.

On my last day at violin school I joined students gathered around

Ardoli as he applied the final coat of varnish to an instrument. Slow and methodical, he worked from left to right, using only the end of the brush to produce a perfectly satisfying, conker gleam. The students watched every tiny move he made, as if they might absorb a skill borne of decades of experience by osmosis. Apprentices to the old masters also learned by watching them at work. And ever since Nicolò Amati began taking on apprentices in the seventeenth century, it has also been part of a luthier's training in Cremona to make copies of old-master instruments. Francesco Ruggieri was one of Amati's first apprentices, and he spent many years refining his skills in this way. He even inscribed Amati's signature on the labels he stuck inside his copied instruments. As time passed, it was inevitable that this practice would begin to cause trouble. The first incident was recorded in the year following Nicolò's death, when a court musician from Mantua called Tommaso Vitali bought what he believed to be a rather expensive Amati violin. It was only when he got it home and examined it more closely that he discovered a second label beneath the first, this one signed by Francesco Ruggieri. Although Ruggieri's instruments are worth a lot of money these days, Vitali had certainly paid well over the odds for an apprentice copy. Outraged, he wrote to his employer asking for help in getting a refund, but history does not relate what happened next.[*]

Students at the violin school still make copies of Old Italians from the Museo del Violino, and when I spotted a sheaf of photographs and minutely measured plans on a desk, I knew I had found a copyist. He had chosen a sixteenth-century tenor viola as his subject. He didn't like it much because its archaic body was so long and its neck so short that playing it would always be uncomfortable. Nevertheless, he was willing to make the whole instrument just for the opportunity to recreate the intricate inlaid patterns on its fingerboard and tailpiece. By now I knew that all the students were obsessed, and obsession is what it takes to succeed in the strange world of violin-making.

[*] W. Henry Hill, Arthur F. Hill and Alfred E. Hill, *Antonio Stradivari: His Life and Work (1644–1737)*, Dover Publications, 1963, p. 211.

Violin A & E

The Difference between Copies and Fakes

Whatever happens to all the copies made of Old Italians over the centuries? Where do they all go? That question was still lodged in my mind long after I left Cremona and came home, so that eventually I couldn't resist pursuing it. I already knew about social hierarchy in the world of violins, because Florian Leonhard had introduced me to its elite at his London office. But if I wanted to investigate this curious new perspective on Old Italians I needed to get away from those cosseted creatures with their rarefied lives, and explore a much broader cross-section of violin society. I decided that an auction would be a good place to see a variety of instruments, but I knew that it would be no good going to grand city auctions, because that is where original Old Italians are sold. Instead I went to an auction deep in the English countryside. Like every auction house I have ever been to outside London, it smelled of bacon butties sold from a hatch, alongside strong tea, chocolate bars and thick slices of fruit-cake. We were in a unit on an industrial estate, and as I climbed the metal steps to the upstairs room where the instruments were displayed for viewing, I expected to hear a cacophony of different violins competing to be heard as they were tried by prospective buyers, but all the instruments lay inert and silent. I was still standing by the door and taking in the quietness of the room when a young Chinese man came over to stand beside me. 'Rubbish,' he said authoritatively, indicating a long table covered in piles of instruments, and then 'not rubbish', pointing at violins and violas lying nose-to-tail on shelves, then at two more long tables stacked with bows and bundles of the pernambuco wood for making them, and finally at cellos standing grandly to attention in a line against the wall. 'Understood,' I said, before he strode off.

In among the instruments in the rubbish range were battered boxes full of pegs, chin rests, tailpieces, bridges and violin-making tools. There were also stacks of reference books, some violin cases, and even a few dubious paintings with violins as their theme. The instruments themselves sported so many kinds of injury and distress that they began to remind me of illustrations in a *First Responders Handbook*. They had cracks in their bellies and holes in their backs, torn f-holes, crackled varnish and missing ribs. A few were only held together by rubber bands and many were missing strings, tailpieces, pegs and even necks. I had stumbled on the perfect school trip for students from Voltini's restoration class in Cremona.

I joined a small group of potential customers circling the table in silence. We were all at violin A & E after some mighty catastrophe, and they were the triage nurses. Every crippled creature held their attention entirely while they examined it, front and back, and as often as not this slow and tender turning between their hands was accompanied by the rattle of a dislodged sound post. Some instruments were factory made, some painfully amateur, and some finely crafted but irrevocably broken. There was a copy of a Guarnerius. It must have fooled someone with its false identity long ago because it had a typewritten letter tucked beneath its sagging strings. 'I am afraid that unless you have a certificate of authenticity this is unlikely to be a Guarneri del Gesù', somebody from Sotheby's had written in 1978. Its owner had clearly lost all interest at that point, for now it lay abandoned like a lost dog in a pound, with its bridge down and most of its strings broken.

You might think this the nadir of violin life, until you saw the cardboard boxes under the table and read the catalogue entries to go with them. In that lower circle of violin hell, the names of Old Italians were everywhere. 'Six various old full-size Stradivarius violins estimate £60–£100', read the catalogue entry for a cardboard box splitting at the seams, and 'Five various full-size violins, including an Amati violin, estimate £100–£150', read another. There was even a 'Stradivarius,

Germany, 1810'. I was sure that all the instruments I pulled out from boxes or carrier bags had been made long after Stradivari's death, when Cremona's lutherie workshops already lay silent and abandoned. They had as much in common with their Old Italian models as 'orange-flavoured drink' has to pure orange juice. Like a herd of decrepit donkeys, these poor old things were fit only to be put out to grass.

On broad shelves along the wall were all the instruments my new Chinese acquaintance had categorized as 'not rubbish'. I felt like a foreigner in their company because they were all German, Austrian or English, and there were no Italian instruments at all. Once, and only once, somebody picked up a beautiful, shabby violin, drew a bow across the strings and coaxed out a faltering phrase. I went over to him and said, 'Does nobody else care about their sound?' He pointed out something I should have noticed for myself – most of the violins were unplayable because their strings were down, and as often as not the sound posts were rattling around inside them. 'But nobody is interested in their voices anyway,' he said, 'because they are all dealers and restorers, none of them are musicians.' For a moment I had a vision of all those mute violins being sold over and over again among dealers, like tools for some arcane trade that nobody had the skills to practise any more. 'I've set my heart on this one,' he said, and I could see why. It was listed as 'Tyrolean, early-18th century, in need of restoration'. 'Will you have it restored?' I asked. 'No,' he replied, and I looked again at the cracks in its belly, and stretches of exposed wood where the varnish had worn away completely from its top. Then I glanced at the holes in the man's jumper and his unwashed hair, and saw a match made in heaven. If there were ever a competition for the violin most like its owner, they would win it together, hands down.

We spoke in hushed voices like everybody else in the room, except for the large bearded man in a beret who had settled into an armchair left over from some earlier sale, grasping a steaming mug of tea in one enormous hand. 'There was this born-again Christian cowboy on the plain,' he began, his voice already convulsed by laughter. A few other dealers gathered round him, but I couldn't wait for the punchline because the bidding was about to begin downstairs. There hadn't been many people at the viewing, and there were even fewer in the auction room. I said as much to the auctioneer, but he told me they had registered over six hundred online bidders.

'Online? How can they bid without handling the instruments for themselves?' I asked, which he clearly considered a naive question.

'If it looks OK in a photograph,' he replied, 'it will probably sound OK. And anyway, if there is some hidden problem, they can always put it into another auction.'

And another and another, like a second-hand car with a fault concealed deep within its wiring. I had one of those once. It would stall in the middle of roundabouts or on crossroads, and nothing on earth would persuade the engine to start again. After too many of these mishaps I put it back in the car auction, and I have felt an uncomfortable mix of guilt and triumph ever since.

The crippled copies with their silly names were the first violins to be sold, and the prices they fetched were a revelation.

'Do I see twenty pounds anywhere? No? Fifteen? Can anyone start me at fifteen?'

There was none of the nail-biting atmosphere of the big auction room during that early stage of the sale, none of the applause, the bitter congratulations or half-hearted handshakes. The box of six 'Stradivarius' violins went for a hundred pounds.

There was hardly anyone in the auction room, but it was clear that the telephone bidders would always be with us, invisible, competitive, persistent, like a family of ambitious ghosts. They chased up the price of the pernambuco bow planks, and when the dark brown, hard-working German and Austrian violins on shelves against the wall were sold, many fetched five figures. For a moment it was almost glamorous in the saleroom, but we soon reconnected with reality, my new friend and I, walking the mile or so back to the country bus stop, our small suitcases rattling behind us over rutted lanes.

*

But what of the other copies of Old Italians, the ones so beautifully and convincingly made by luthiers all over the world that you might wonder if being genuinely old or even Italian really mattered any more? Customers for these instruments are often top musicians who usually play an Old Italian that they have on loan from a bank, a foundation or a private investor. The copies they commission of these instruments are a practical antidote to the very real anxiety that their violins' true owners might reclaim them at any time. Others like to use a copy while working abroad, especially if they are going to a country where it can be difficult to leave with an antique in your luggage, even if it was there when you arrived. And finally, some like to have a spare instrument as back-up, because their hard-working Old Italians are antiques, and they often have to slip away for maintenance and repair.

Luthiers making copies at this level will have measured the original instrument exhaustively, taken colour photographs of it from every angle, both inside and out, and cut templates with a laser so that they can reproduce the exact shape of its arching. Some will also have a UV scan made of the varnish, or even a full-body CT scan. These luthiers aren't attempting to trick anyone; they're simply trying to create instruments with some of the same qualities as a Cremona violin for musicians who could never afford an original.

When it comes to selecting the resonance wood that will do so much to determine the instrument's sound, these luthiers will often choose Alpine spruce from the same high-altitude forests as Guarneri del Gesù or Stradivari. For some of them the tone of an Old Italian can only be explained by the gentle decay that has broken down starches in the cell walls of old resonance wood. They try to reproduce this effect by steaming or boiling the new spruce they plan to use for the copy. Others even go so far as to trigger genuine rot in fresh spruce by incubating it with real fungi, specially selected for its ability to break down cellulose and hemicellulose. Some luthiers take another direction by choosing to mimic the conditions imposed on timber when it was floated downriver from the Alps to

Venice. Long soaking makes the wood flexible and speeds up the seasoning process by diluting the sugary sap in the cells. However, none of these arduous and carefully calibrated processes can be guaranteed to produce that elusive 'Old Italian' sound.

I don't know if Melvin Goldsmith has ever experimented with cooking or rotting, but he is said to be one of very few luthiers in the world who can make copies of old violins from Cremona that not only look like the originals, but speak like them as well. When I visited him he was living in Essex, close to the farm where he grew up, where the glint of water is on every horizon. His workshop in the corner of a barn was a small, dim, perfectly tidy room with a workbench worn shiny along one wall, and a neat arrangement of tools above it. He told me straight away that most of the tools had belonged to his grandfather, an amateur violin-maker who taught him to make his first instrument when he was only twelve years old. But that was that, because afterwards Melvin was on his own. While his friends were outside playing football, he would be indoors making violin after violin, or studying old-instrument sale catalogues from Sotheby's. Of course he made mistakes, but that was easily resolved. He just hung unsuccessful instruments on the washing line in the garden and shot them with his air rifle. Despite being entirely self-taught, Melvin is often described these days as one of the best luthiers of his generation. But he is very wary of flattering judgements. 'In my job,' he says, 'if you start to believe that sort of thing, if you don't stay humble, it trips you up.'

Melvin's most successful instruments are made using resonance wood that is already about three hundred years old. When he first embarked on using antique wood he began his search for it in the way that a search for anything begins these days – online. It didn't take him long to find a violin-wood dealer in Italy with a few pieces to sell and he bought the lot, sight unseen. When they arrived, the pieces of wood were very dirty on the outside, as if they had been stored in the open air, but they were so pale and clean on the inside that Melvin guessed they were probably only about fifty years old. Nevertheless, he photographed the tree-ring patterns on a couple of them and sent the images off to the dendrochronologist Peter Ratcliff for testing. The results were so exciting that Peter rang him up on a Sunday afternoon. One of the pieces of wood came from a tree felled in 1708, and the other from 1719. And when Peter compared their ring patterns to those on his database, he found they were the same as those on some of Stradivari's violins. This was startling news: it meant the wood Melvin had bought so casually online came from the same tree that Stradivari used to make some of his instruments, or at least a tree that grew very close to it.

What could be better than making a copy from the same wood as Stradivari? And yet, according to modern theory, the pieces of wood were both too dense and too brittle to use for resonance wood. Fortunately Melvin is a free spirit, as free as he was as a child, working in complete isolation, and he discovered that instead of making the wood unworkable, these qualities made it intensely responsive. 'And now that I had started using old wood that didn't conform to modern theories,' he explained, 'I made better instruments than I had ever done by following conventional rules.' In fact, one of the pieces of wood turned out to be so responsive that the violin he made from it had the best tone of any he had ever produced. It was a copy of a Guarneri del Gesù that once belonged to the great violinist Fritz Kreisler. These days the *Kreisler* belongs to the Danish government, which loans it to the acclaimed concertmaster and conductor Nikolaj Znaider. What a strange situation. Melvin had been commissioned to make a copy of the *Kreisler* by a player in another leading orchestra, but of course Znaider was so busy playing it that Melvin never got the opportunity he needed to spend time taking measurements and absorbing the essence of the instrument. Eventually Znaider invited him to come to Valencia, where the *Kreisler* would be idling away its mornings while he rehearsed the orchestra. Melvin packed up his tools and set off for Valencia. 'It felt a bit like setting off on a pilgrimage,' he told me, 'because I was going to meet Guarneri del Gesù, Kreisler and Znaider all at once, and I was quite nervous.'

For four hours each morning the *Kreisler* lay on a polystyrene

platform, like a patient on an examination table, while Melvin measured the thickness of its wood with a magnetic gauge, made
measurements of every other dimension and photographed it
exhaustively. He couldn't take the strings off and so he had to cut a
template of the arching by eye, slip it under the strings and shave
the card with a knife until it fitted perfectly.

It took him five days to summon up enough courage to ask
Znaider if he could try the *Kreisler* himself, and his description of
the experience is the only answer I will ever need to the question of
what makes an Old Italian special. When Melvin held it in his arms,
his first impression was of eagerness, as if it were starting to make
a sound even before he drew the bow across the strings. And when
he did start to play, he said it was as powerful and as responsive as a
racehorse, and so loud that it sounded almost like an electric instrument. He already had all the measurements he needed to make a
copy, but at that moment he knew there was also an intangible quality to the *Kreisler*, something almost supernatural that he doubted
he could ever capture. Many months later, Melvin gave Nikolaj
Znaider the opportunity to try the copy he had made. The fact that
Znaider, who had been playing the original *Kreisler* for years, immediately commissioned another copy for himself tells us all we
need to know.

Most large families have a few shady relations, and when it comes
to Old Italians, it's the copies made to deceive that let the family
down. The practice of meddling with the labels on Old Italians can
be traced back to Tarisio, who had no compunction about replacing
a disappointing label with something more auspicious, or altering
the date on an existing label. According to Florian Leonhard, it can
be very difficult to spot a false label, although he will look for signs
in the quality of the paper, the way it has aged, the depth of the
impression made on it by the print, the era of the font used in the
printing, and the label's position in the instrument. His examin-
ations sometimes reveal labels that were produced on laser-jet
printers, sometimes early twentieth-century screen prints, and
sometimes even eighteenth-century facsimiles made only fifty years

after the instrument itself.* According to Leonhard, the most difficult fakes to spot are the ones created from a violin that was
originally made as the copy of an older instrument. It might have
been created in all innocence a hundred years ago, but when a dealer
distresses, retouches or even revarnishes it, it will start to look very
much older than it is. 'Those are the dangerous fakes,' Leonhard
says, 'and it requires a bit more skill to spot them. You have to see
through many layers of faking and distinguish between repairs and
reworkings.'†

Dodgy dealers create glamorous stories full of erudition and lies
to accompany the fakes they slip into the world. However, there are
some things they cannot invent or conceal. Dendrochronology will
always expose the lies of a dealer claiming a violin is older than it is.
And violins have another, even more subtle way of preserving their
true pasts in their bodies. It was Florian Leonhard who explained
this to me, using an unexpected analogy between violins and the
production of Wagyu beef in Japan. 'They massage those cows
every day,' he said, 'and it makes their meat incredibly tender.' I
started telling him about eating Wagyu beef in Japan myself, holding it between chopsticks and dipping it into the boiling oil over a
small burner brought to our restaurant table. I am not much of a
meat eater, but I certainly remember the almost disturbing tender-
ness of the flesh from those cosseted cows. However, it soon became
clear that cooking and eating were both irrelevant to Leonhard's
analogy, because he went on to explain that much the same thing
happens to a violin when a good musician plays it, and the vibrations of the strings running through its body massage the wood and
teach the cells how to move together. The way a violin vibrates is
the key to its sound and, as it never forgets what it has learned, it
will continue to carry the imprint of former players in its voice, and

---

* Florian Leonhard, 'Florian Leonhard on a Mysterious Violin and the Process
of Authentication', *Strings* magazine, 7 December 2016. https://bit.ly/2NoDf9d
† Femke Colborne, 'Can you Tell a Fake Instrument from the Genuine
Article?', *The Strad*, 6 August 2019. https://bit.ly/2QhU6tA

perhaps even a memory of their music as well. Leonhard told me that some of the instruments he handles are so deeply inscribed with the legacies of extraordinary musicians that a violinist trying one for the first time will sometimes say that it seems to be willing her to play it in a certain way, as if it wanted to slip back into the routines and practices of its last owner.

Among all of the generations of musicians who must have owned Lev's violin since it was made, adding their layers of influence to its sound, choosing where it lived, deciding what jobs it took, how often it was restored, how much it travelled, and when it was played, there were only two I could ever hope to talk to. By now I had already spoken to Greg many times, and so my next task was to contact Lev, the Russian musician who had lent and eventually sold Greg the violin. When we spoke for the first time it was on the phone, and Lev suggested almost at once that I come to Glasgow and meet him for coffee. I have turned down more substantial invitations in London, which is much closer to home, and yet I was so caught up in the story of his old violin that I didn't hesitate before saying yes to coffee in a city over three hundred miles away. We arranged to meet close to the Conservatoire, and as Lev walked towards me down Renfrew Street, with sunlight illuminating his hair, I wondered yet again why we women dye ours, when so many of us could be wearing glamorous silver crowns like Lev. If you remember my description of Greg, you may start to think his violin has belonged only to men with exceptional hair. Maybe so. I don't think Lev's has altered in much but colour since he was a child. It is a thick, gleaming, neatly parted thatch, worn low over a pair of startlingly large almond eyes. We went straight to a café, where Lev perched on the edge of his seat, starting to talk at once in his soft Russian voice, as if he had been waiting a long time for this opportunity to reminisce about an old friend. 'I only ever had one violin like it,' he said immediately. 'It has amazing power, even though it is quite small, and an extraordinary tone, a mellowness about the lower strings that's like nothing else in the world.' It was such a relief to hear him say that, for it seemed to justify all the time I had devoted to following the story unspooling from that glorious sound.

'I suppose that's not surprising when you consider it was made in Cremona,' I said.

'Cremona?' he exclaimed. 'I've never thought it was from Cremona, but I can tell you where I found it.'

Lev explained he was still living in southern Russia when he bought the violin from the old Roma musician at the market in Rostov-on-Don. He played it in Rostov for a decade or so before he and his wife Julia emigrated from Russia, first to America and then to Scotland, a decade within living memory, a decade that could be tracked and traced in ways more literal than anything I had done in the service of this story before. When coffee time merged into sandwich time at the tables all around us, Lev invited me to join him and Julia for a late lunch at home. I still don't find it easy to explain exactly what happened next, but for anybody who knows her, it might be enough to say 'Julia', who is an ambassador for every kind of cultural exchange between Glasgow and its twin city, Rostov-on-Don. Until that day Greg had been my only ally and confidant when it came to Lev's violin. Now there was Julia, with her bright clothes, glittering rings and black hair streaked with cobalt blue to match her eyes. She seemed to take it for granted I would want to go to Russia to find out more about the place her husband's violin had lived and the music it played, and while chopping vegetables and tossing them into a hot pan, she cooked up a travel plan as though that were just as easy as making soup. It would be neither safe nor fruitful to go to Russia alone, she said, and as Lev would be caught up in rehearsals and teaching commitments, she offered herself as my minder, fixer and translator. As she got up to make coffee, Julia began to talk about visas and flights, as if my decision had already been made. Again, she offered to do all the donkey work, finding the cheapest and most direct route to Rostov and arranging my visa, so that going to Russia began to seem almost as simple as staying at home.

When I began following the story of Italian violins – and of Lev's violin in particular – I expected them to take me ever deeper into Italy. And they did, for a while. But then they began leading me on vicarious journeys to unexpected destinations in other countries, such as the opera house in eighteenth-century Prague, violin dealers' shops in nineteenth-century Paris, and Second World War concentration camps. Now I was being offered a literal journey that could take me out of Europe all together. I hesitated – of course I did – and yet I had never forgotten the Klezmer music Lev's violin played on that summer night years before. It is common property these days, but Klezmer was originally the sound of celebration among Yiddish-speaking Ashkenazi Jews. And somewhere deep within the music that entranced me that night were tunes spanning the great distance between the beginning of this story in Italy and the life of Lev's violin in Russia. Why? Because some of the first Ashkenazi to settle in Europe went to northern Italy in the ninth century. Embedded in the music that had me dancing on that first night was the memory of tunes that Ashkenazi fiddlers played centuries ago in Italian courts, inns and market towns, and carried with them as they drifted east towards the Russian Empire. Between the end of the eighteenth century and the First World War, Jews were forced to live in the Pale of Settlement, and then Klezmer became the sound of celebration in their muddy, smoky villages. Without fiddles there were no tunes, and so into the morass of possible explanations for the arrival of Lev's violin in Russia, I tossed the idea of a Jewish musician travelling east from Italy to Russia.

And for all of these reasons I found myself on a plane to Russia.

Smuggled

Lev's Violin in the USSR

Aeroflot had delivered me to Moscow in the middle of the night. I could find nowhere to buy the comfort of a cup of coffee while I waited for my connecting flight to Rostov-on-Don, although I could have bought any number of Russian dolls, as if this urgent need must be met day and night. As I sat yawning and shivering on a grey plastic chair, it struck me that a neat little Russian doll might be a good analogy for the experience I expected to have while I was in Rostov. I had always seen the story of Lev's violin as a great big tatty parcel wrapped in layer upon layer of paper. Learning each new thing about it felt like tearing off one of those layers to discover another chapter of the story underneath, so that eventually it came to feel as if I were playing my own version of that children's party game pass-the-parcel. I expected things to be very different in Rostov, because instead of relying on a story I could speak to real people, visit real places where Lev had gone with his violin, and perhaps even hear the kind of music they played together. In that state between sleeping and waking, I imagined the information I would uncover being as fresh as the scent of the wood inside a Russian doll, as bright as the paint on its exterior, and as precise as the sharp edges of the two halves as they snapped shut.

Our plane emerged from thick cloud above Rostov at dawn. It was already late November and I had expected snow, but instead I saw a swathe of wet fields under a grit-grey sky. Ours was the only plane on the tarmac, although we taxied past rows of drones, where soldiers in fur hats stood about in small groups, chatting like men at a car auction. It wasn't difficult to spot Julia in the arrivals hall, because she and her old friend Gregor were the only people there.

Gregor – or Grisha as Julia told me to call him – was our self-appointed driver, and although I didn't know it yet, I would be spending so much time on the neatly carpeted back seat of his 1970s Mercedes that it would come to feel like home. Julia had arrived a few days ahead of me. Her phone rang several times as we drove towards the city. After one call she turned right round in her seat to say, 'I've told everyone that you are coming to find out about Lev's violin, and now they keep ringing me to ask if Agatha Christie has arrived yet.'

Julia had booked rooms for us in the hotel where Lev used to play his violin in a club on the sixth floor. Every week he would tuck an embroidered Cossack shirt into his trousers, tuck his trousers into his Cossack boots, and take part in a variety show for foreign visitors. At weekends Lev earned extra cash by playing at parties and weddings with an Armenian band. These were very different undertakings to his day job as the viola player in the Rostov String Quartet. Throughout his musical training at school and conservatoire Lev had been a violinist, but it was a viola player that the quartet needed, and this opportunity was too good to miss. You would never expect a quartet to be your only form of employment in the West, but in the Soviet Union Lev and his colleagues were paid a full-time salary to work together every day, taking each piece of music they practised apart, note by note, before putting it back together and playing it with absolute precision. Uri, Sasha, Leonid and Lev, the four of them were young, ambitious, diligent and talented. They had studied under the greatest quartet teachers in the world, and now they had established very Soviet careers, combining regular concerts for workers in factory canteens with triumphs such as winning the grand prize in the Borodin All-Soviet Competition in 1983.

The entire crew of some enormous ship was checking out when we arrived at our hotel. With their stripy T-shirts, bulky parkas and fur hats, they looked like handsome extras in a film about naval history. We joined them in the long queue at reception and when our turn eventually came I asked for a map of the city. They didn't have one. No tourists, just sailors, I suppose, and perhaps sailors don't need maps. To be in an unknown city without a map renders you utterly powerless, but I didn't care because I thought I'd soon be creating my own map of Rostov, plotted on the life of Lev's violin.

My room on the eighth floor overlooked a small park. Normally it would have been virtually empty at that time of year, but the weather was so mild that it was still full of life. From my window that week I was able to gauge the daily progress of a puppy learning to walk on the lead, see the same groups of stray cats or dogs, crows and schoolchildren convene each morning, and watch the same man going through the litter bins on his way to bed at night. Julia and I met downstairs for a coffee. Where should we start? When I met Lev in Glasgow he told me about buying his violin from a gypsy in some quiet corner of Rostov market. This was the first chapter in a real history of Lev's violin, and so that is where we chose to begin.

Grisha drove, sweeping up a side street in his magnificent old Merc and parking jauntily askew on the pavement. We strolled through the square in front of the cathedral and made our way to a canvas-covered city of stalls. The day was dull and mild, and yet the place was illuminated by the vivid colours of apples, tomatoes, cucumbers, onions, plums and pears, pickled whole and in their skins, of beetroot and filigree piles of shredded cabbage and carrot, piled high on every stall. Some people sold nothing but pomegranates; some sold homemade sauces in any bottle they could find, and others depended on cranberries for a living. Their stalls were packed with jam-jar measures priced at 50, 100 or 200 roubles and overflowing with berries the colour of arterial blood. There were stalls for local sunflower oils that had been decanted into vodka or brandy bottles, each one a more or less tawny shade of gold. Wherever we paused, we were offered a drop of oil to taste on the backs of our hands. Each one was distinctive, rich, nutty and unexpectedly delicious. We stopped by stall after stall to taste some speciality spooned in a generous dollop into our hands. 'All one the same,' Grisha grumbled, as we accepted a fourth and then a fifth version of pickled cabbage, 'only price change.' But how wrong he was. Rostov was once a busy port, trading in Siberian furs, caviar from

Astrakhan, Turkish tobacco, iron from the Urals, grain and smoked fish, and it has always been a multi-ethnic place. The River Don marks the boundary between East and West, so that, when I stood on its banks, I realized that following Lev's violin had brought me to the very edge of Europe. Bearing all this ethnic and geographical variety in mind, it's no wonder every version of a pickle in the market is subtly sharper, sweeter, crisper or softer than the last. Grisha stood by as we bought a plastic box full of glistening red peppers, another of aubergine slices rolled tight around a stuffing of ground walnuts, and some pickled cabbage. Beaming women parked themselves in my path as we left the stalls. They were from northern Russia, Grisha said, mushroom country. It was mild that afternoon but nevertheless they were swathed in scarves and swaddled in thick coats, and they had strings of dried mushrooms pinned to their sleeves. They turned slowly on the spot, arms outstretched, like dumpy, animated Christmas trees. I would probably have bought some mushrooms from them, but Julia was discouraging because they were northern mushrooms: she neither knew what they were called nor how to use them.

We climbed the stairs to the cheese market, where everything was white, the buckets of sour cream, the cooked yoghurt, kefir and mounds of cottage cheese. We could have filled up again on all the samples offered of this new take on white goods. In another part of the market were stalls piled high with heaps of dried apricots, apple rings, halved pears, cranberries, barberries, pineapple rings, prunes and figs, sacks of fresh hazelnuts and walnuts, vats of shiny sultanas and raisins. An Uzbek boy weighed up a bag of blond raisins for me, told me it would cost 800 roubles, added another scoopful and charged me 500 roubles. This made his stall irresistible and so I bought a bit of everything, but when I got it home at last it all tasted of one thing – woodsmoke.

There had been few scents on the cool, grey air, but then we came to the fish stalls and the smell hit hard. In the second half of the nineteenth century – when Rostov was both the biggest port and the biggest railway junction in the south of Russia – caviar and local fish were shipped north through Rostov to the inland markets of the empire. In those days the fish was either smoked or put on ice, unlike the lively pike, sturgeon and catfish thrashing in the shallows of plastic boxes all around me, their water supposedly aerated by a rusty oxygen cylinder behind each stall. There were boxes of wriggling crayfish beside them, their beady black eyes shining. Crustaceans are wasted on me. I don't enjoy the intimacy of pulling off their legs, and prising away their shells seems a gross intrusion on their privacy. Saw off this and suck it, lever out that and lick it, I just don't like it at all. And yet freshwater crayfish are a treat in any country, and I was ashamed of myself later that week when Julia's friends invited us over for dinner. I just couldn't do justice to the gigantic bowl they set down in front of me, brimming over with those familiar little bodies, their eyes so black and beady that it was as if boiling hadn't bothered them at all.

Every stall in the fish market was decorated with golden bouquets of dried and smoked fish, iridescent in the light of a naked bulb. Asking for a delectable taste of any preserved fish always triggered the same operation, a subtle incision performed with a penknife's fine blade beneath a fin. 'Before the Revolution,' Julia said, as I popped a sliver of fish into my mouth, 'there was so much fish in the Don that people used to dry it and use it instead of firewood. But under the Soviet Union the river was poisoned by industrial waste, and it's never been the same again.' 'Mmmm, thanks Julia.'

The main market, with its conical hills of dried fruit, sock stalls, hat stalls, knife stalls and piles of stacked saucepans, would never have been the place to sell a violin. But then we went out to the *tolkuchka*, the flea market on the tram tracks outside, where the cathedral's gilded domes illuminate the sky, the congregation mixes with the real bargain hunters, and everyone is equal when it comes to being run over by a tram. A very old woman, her feet on the tracks, offered broken tubes and boxes of household poisons from a cardboard tray. A shopping spree there could eliminate the wasps, cockroaches, rats and ants in your life – and perhaps you as well.

Opposite her someone had made a nest from a few upturned knit-
ted hats inside a cardboard box, and filled it with a tangle of stray
kittens that she arranged and rearranged constantly, attempting to
create an impression of sweetness from their skinny bodies and
mangy faces. Someone else was trying to sell a plump Pekinese
puppy, wearing it in the meantime like a sash across her broad
chest. It was in this liminal place, among unwanted pets, bunches of
fresh dill, radishes and broken radios, that Lev might have spotted
an old man selling junk from the pavement. I saw someone very
similar by the tram tracks, and he'd not got much to offer, just a
dented kettle, a cup and a pair of army boots with holes in them.
Lev probably had no need of another violin, least of all a dirty one
with no strings. But like a man who surrounds himself with dogs, or
has so many children that one more will make no difference, he
would have begun, almost automatically, to embark on a bargaining
strategy. He would have checked the kettle for leaks, held the broken
boots to his feet as if trying them for size, and enquired after a sau-
cer for the chipped cup before eventually making an offer on the
violin. He could have bought the kettle for the same price, for in
that place usefulness was the only criterion of worth, and he left the
market with the violin under his arm. It had come into his life as
casually as a stray cat slipping through the back door, but he recognized it immediately as an exceptional instrument.

Most of Lev's work with the violin was for the Armenian wedding band, but winter is not the season for weddings in any country,
and Julia had to dream up other ways of introducing me to the
Armenian diaspora and their music in Rostov. Her introduction
began rather unexpectedly as we were speeding through late-night
traffic on the way back to our hotel. Or that is what I thought we
were doing, until another of the kind friends Julia had called on to
pack us into their cars and drive us wherever the violin led, glanced
over his shoulder and said loudly, 'Is very exciting moment for you,
Helena. Now we go see theatre shaped like tractor!' And so we did,
gazing at it from the middle of a colossal square, surrounded by the
swirling lights of the traffic, coffee carts, pickpockets and groups

of young men. Julia's friend was anxious about leaving his car unguarded in that place, but I could do nothing about my slow progress when it came to recognizing the building's tractor shape, for it was not constructed to the plan of any tractor I had ever seen. Julia and her friend studied me, I studied the building, and the traffic kept on roaring past. 'Can you see it now, Helena?' 'Not really,' and 'not really' again, but then I realized it had taken the archetypal Soviet tractor with caterpillar tracks as its model. 'I get it!' I shouted, and we all hurried back to the car and drove away. On our way back to the hotel Julia explained that until 1930 there had been nothing but wheat fields on the site of the tractor and the square in front of it, and that this open space had been the frontier between the city of Rostov and an Armenian settlement called Nor Nakhichevan (or 'new' Nakhichevan, to distinguish it from Nakhichevan in Azerbaijan). The following day we retraced our route across the square with theatre-shaped-like-tractor, crossing the old frontier again on our way to the Museum of Russian–Armenian Friendship.

Nor Nakhichevan was absorbed into the rest of Rostov in 1928, and yet I knew we had arrived because it still felt like a very distinctive place. The main streets and squares were lined with imposing nineteenth-century churches, houses, theatres and schools. Poplar trees had scattered the pavements with butter-coloured leaves, and pots of geraniums in windows and porches lent a blaze of colour to the thin winter light. The museum was in a handsome nineteenth-century building. Inside, we had the curator to ourselves. She could speak English but much preferred not to, so that poor Julia had the job of translating everything she told us about her ancestral history. While she talked I looked around me at all the paintings of famous authors, politicians, teachers and scientists who had lived in Nor Nakhichevan over the years, at glass cases full of traditional Armenian tools, utensils and musical instruments, at national costumes, spinning wheels and books. Every single object in the museum had its own story to tell, just like Lev's violin, all of them valid, fascinating and clamouring to be heard. Take the *tar*. It was a stringed instrument, but its narrow body and elegant long neck reminded me more of an egret than a violin. And given the chance, it would have told a very different story, because while luthiers all over Europe spent the sixteenth, seventeenth and eighteenth centuries refining the engineering and design of violins, *tars* continued to be crudely cobbled together from unseasoned wood. And while violins were taking sophisticated audiences by storm at courts and in cathedrals and opera houses, Armenian farmers and labourers were using *tars* to play their unselfconscious music in fields and villages.

Among all the different communities in Rostov, there was a particularly strong bond between the Armenians and the Jews. They had lived alongside each other for at least two hundred years, and so it was inevitable that Jewish and Armenian musicians would play together, exchanging tunes and absorbing them into their own repertoires. It was also inevitable that Armenian bands would be invited to perform at Jewish weddings, where the guests would never have been satisfied with music that did not include the sound of a fiddle. This must have happened so often that a Jewish fiddle player – like Lev – soon became an essential member of any Armenian band. This local peculiarity has never been recorded in any official history of Armenian music, and yet it is so familiar to the local community in Rostov that it passes without comment.

The wedding band Lev used to play with was long gone, but one day Julia said she had been able to revive her connection with an Armenian couple whose wedding they played at in about 1981. The groom had clearly put the intervening years to good use. 'He is an oligarch now,' Julia said, 'and so you will never be able to meet him.' However, Julia, who should run workshops in lateral thinking, had asked if we could see a copy of the video made of his wedding, as this would allow me to see Lev's violin playing in the band. The prospect hovered over us all week. It was a very big favour to ask on behalf of a stranger, and as this oligarch wasn't a man for answering messages, all we could do was wait. One day, however, we got back to the hotel to find an envelope waiting for Julia at reception. Inside it was the wedding video copied on to two DVDs. 'I think we should send him one of the bottles of whisky you brought with you,' Julia said. The whisky was single malt, but even so I knew it wouldn't meet oligarch standards. Nevertheless, we sent it off to him in a taxi.

If I tell you that asking for an Armenian bride's hand in marriage, getting engaged, getting married, and the marriage celebrations are all staging posts on a journey that can last for days, and that almost every moment of every stage must be accompanied by music and dancing, you will understand why Lev had said that he worried about his stamina when they invited him to join the band. The cameraman had begun recording in the morning, when the band accompanied the groom and a few women from his family as they danced through the sunny streets of Nor Nakhichevan to the bride's house. I saw Lev striding along behind them. Of course he looked younger than he does today, but curiously, the violin gleaming in the autumn sunshine looked younger too. We saw the bride's family spill out of the gates to welcome the groom, and then, like un-invited guests, we slipped in behind the musicians and watched the groom's elder brother ask the bride's family for her hand. As that carefully choreographed day went on, we were always in the right place at the right time. We hovered at the bedroom door with a crowd of other women to catch a glimpse of the bride in an explosion of frills, and then followed the hooting cavalcade of wedding cars moving slowly but unstoppably through Nor Nakhichevan's narrow streets. The wedding ceremony was long, and yet we hung on to see the bride and groom crowned as rulers of their new household, and we were already in place for their triumphant return from church. We saw the tables laden with food and cornucopias of grapes and pomegranates, the tired children and the tearful uncle, the ebullient aunts, the cook in her apron, and the bride and groom dancing in a narrow space between the tables. Hands lifted, wrists perpetually turning, they gripped wads of banknotes that guests slipped between their fingers. Darkness fell at last over the long day, the groom lit a cigarette and the camera suddenly focused on Lev's violin, for throughout every phase of the ceremonies and celeb-rations the music had been as reliable and relentless as waves on a shore. It was clear from the start that those Armenian musicians were no purists, for they were playing none of the instruments I had seen in the museum in Nor Nakhichevan. They had a clarinet instead of the traditional *duduk* or *zurna*, the drum was not a *dhol*, there were two accordions and Lev with his violin. There was nothing purist about their repertoire either. Lev launched into an Armenian tune, but before long it morphed into a Klezmer one, then a song from Georgia and a gypsy rhythm, before turning Moldavian and then Armenian again. Together Lev's violin and the other instruments wove a wonderfully generic, pan-Caucasian fusion of irresistible, non-stop dance music. And if those epic weekend weddings left any imprint on its voice, I know now that it would only be the cry of a party animal, the clamour of an international jukebox, of a money-spinning dance machine and a full-throttle jubilation generator.

Lev had fallen out of touch with the Armenian musicians in the band long ago, but Julia was not going to be defeated, and by the end of the week she had somehow managed to arrange a meeting with the clarinet player. We gathered in the vast restaurant of a hotel on the edge of an Armenian village outside Rostov. There were only three other people in a room built for celebration: the waiter, an Armenian woman called Yelena who was an old school-friend of Julia's, and a quiet Armenian friend of hers with gold front teeth and tired eyes. Soon there was food on the table in front of us, a jug of fresh cranberries, crushed just enough to release a little juice, and a bottle of vodka. Yelena set the tone with a toast to friendship. 'It's easy to give up your life for a friend,' she said, 'but hard to find a friend you want to give up your life for.' I jumped on the bandwagon, 'to new friends' I said firmly, and I could sense Julia's eyes on me, watching to be sure I followed her instructions by breathing out before downing another glass of vodka, and out again after swallowing it. Julia and Yelena scuttled outside for a cigarette, and when they got back Yelena was ready for another toast. 'Friends are like pebbles on a beach,' she said, 'some fall through your fingers, and others are just too big to drop, so you have to hold on to

them for ever.' That was when Misha, the clarinet player, arrived. He
seemed thrilled to see Julia, and he pulled out his wallet to give her
his card, so they could never lose touch again. The wallet was held
together with several rubber bands that he removed quickly before
extracting the card. When Yelena demanded one for herself, Misha
had to remove the rubber bands all over again, and somehow he
made it seem laborious this time. Yelena and Julia had known each
other a long time. I wondered if they had always competed over
boys. In old friendships some things never change, and it was defin-
itely round one to Julia that night. Misha remembered Lev perfectly.
'We were lucky to have him,' he said, 'because Lev was the literate one, the only one with a musical education.' Then Misha
climbed up to the balcony above the restaurant and began to play
his clarinet just for us, against a backing tape and drum. Yelena
and Julia both hit the floor and danced together in that vast space.
Dari dari dam, dari dari dam said the sweet voice of Misha's clarinet, while Yelena pulled her fingers through her hair and ran her
hands over her hips with the passion of a teenager, and I sat
quietly beside her silent friend and chewed on cranberry juice as
thick as pudding.

Lev had owned the violin for a decade or so by the time he and
Julia decided to emigrate to Boston in 1990. Although Mikhail Gor-
bachev's reforms had made emigration slightly easier by that time,
it was still difficult for an old violin to leave the Soviet Union. The
state classified any violin made before 1870 as antique, and émigré
families were denied the right to take antiques with them when
they left. At first glance this might seem a reasonable way of protecting Russia's national heritage. In practice, however, it doubled as
a system for getting objects to do the state's dirty work, rather as
the Nazis had done by confiscating violins from Jewish musicians
during the Second World War. In this case, the state was denying
émigré musicians the possibility of finding work when they arrived
in their new home, which Lev had described as a way of retaining
control over them after they left the country. When we talked about
it in Glasgow, he was still full of anger and dismay about this

process. 'I had paid the equivalent of seven annual salaries for the viola I played in the quartet,' he said, 'so you can imagine how much it meant to me. Obviously I couldn't pay for it all at once, so I worked and worked and paid over three or four years, but now the state said it was theirs. How could that be?' No wonder Soviet musicians found so many ways to smuggle their instruments out of the country.

Émigrés from Rostov generally packed the possessions they were allowed to take with them into wooden crates for shipping. The bigger the crate, the more it cost to send, but you could put whatever you liked inside, just as long as it wasn't an antique. When their emigration papers finally came through, Lev and Julia had to decide how on earth they were going to get his instruments out of the country, and what other possessions they should take with them. However, Lev's first challenge was to find enough planks to make a packing crate. 'I have never understood,' he once told me, 'why a country with so many forests should be short of wood.' But that was the case, and eventually he had to go to a cemetery to beg for some coffin planks. 'What do you want them for, has someone died?' the officials at the cemetery asked. They didn't seem to think Lev's answer about using coffin planks to make a packing crate would sit well in their paperwork, and so, making it up as they went along, they wrote 'ritual purposes' under the 'Use' section on their form. Lev was bemused. 'What ritual purposes?' he asked. 'Oh goodness knows,' they said, 'but you Jews are always doing strange things and nobody understands what you are up to, so "ritual purposes" will be just fine.' And that was that.

What should they put in the crate? That was the question Lev and Julia wrestled with for weeks. When I look around me at the drifts of possessions that have accumulated in our house, I have no idea what I would choose to take with me as I launched into a brand-new existence. I will always regard some of the things I live with as belonging to my parents or my parents-in-law. Others have been abandoned here in bedrooms and attics by our children, and some we are storing, seemingly for ever, for relations on the move.

And then there are our things, my things, things I have neither had to evaluate nor do without. I have noticed that these objects make peaceful possessions, because they have none of the sentimental charge of the ones I knew as a child. However, their turn will come, because I am sure they are already sinking their talons into the emotions of the next generation. And I have learned from clearing my mother's house that some of the things I like most – because they are worn by age and use – will soon begin to look a little bit disgusting to that new generation. Out of all these things, I have no idea which could stand alone to remind me of my identity and history. What would I have packed into that small wooden box to take away with me to a new life? I don't know because I have lived too long in this clutter without ever needing to ask what matters to me most.

When he looks back on the decisions he and Julia made about packing, Lev says, 'We were like two new-born babies, because we knew nothing about the wider world, or what we might need to survive in it. We had never even had a bank account.' Of course there were plenty of rumours about what they might need in the United States, and they listened to all of them. Most people said it was important to take bedding, and so in the end much of the space in their box was taken up by blankets.

All émigrés were required to pack their crates in the customs yard, and Julia still remembers how bleak that was. 'It was as cold as the railway station of a gulag,' she told me. 'The only difference was Rostov on the other side of the fence, instead of Siberia.' A customs officer had to approve every item before it was packed, but occasionally he would be called away, and that was the moment to slip something into a crate unseen. People often smuggled things out for each other, vital things like musical instruments, and smaller objects like the silver spoons given to babies and passed between the generations of Jewish families, or pieces of jewellery that might not be worth much, but were full of sentimental value for their owners.

When it came to smuggling his violin out of the country, all Lev could do was let down the strings, give it a kiss, slip it in among clothes, quilts and books, and hope for the best. And that is how Lev's violin left Rostov, a stowaway smuggled out among the intimate belongings of some obliging family whose crate was shipped to Israel. And as for me, I left Rostov one day before dawn. Julia was still asleep, but she had ordered a cab for me the night before, and it was soon clear that the booking had come with a set of instructions the driver was intent on following to the letter. My dawn was his dusk and he was in garrulous mood. He drove me down empty roads to the airport, talking all the way, and sometimes we understood each other. When we got there he jumped out and took the fare, but instead of handing over my case as I expected, he led me inside and stood by with a solicitous expression on his face while I checked in. That done, I really expected him to leave, but now he walked me to the Departures gate, where he took both my hands in his own and shook them firmly. When I glanced back over my shoulder he was still there, and still waving enthusiastically. Sometimes I still wonder what Julia said to him. 'Make sure she gets off safely,' perhaps? He certainly knew how to do a job properly.

All the players in the Rostov String Quartet left the Soviet Union at about the same time as Lev, but they sometimes came together for performances. In 1991 they were invited to go to Glasgow and take part in a festival marking the centenary of Prokofiev's birth. Of course Lev was playing viola in the quartet, and so he left his violin behind in Boston. Nevertheless, this was the beginning of a process that would eventually see him bring his violin to Glasgow and open up the next chapter of its life.

It all started at the end-of-festival party in another musician's house. The rooms were crowded, the atmosphere jubilant, and there was a little dog darting among people's legs. Overexcited, overwrought, or perhaps still only a puppy, it began to tear up a newspaper that had fallen on the floor. Someone retrieved the paper, and scanning the shredded 'Situations Vacant' page, noticed an advertisement for the post of First Viola player with Scottish Opera. 'Why don't you apply, Lev?' said all his Scottish friends, and before long someone had made a phone call and arranged an audition before he caught his flight back to Boston the following day. Greg, a member of the Scottish Opera orchestra at that time, was chosen to audition him. When Lev succeeded in getting the job his violin emigrated once again, this time from Boston to Glasgow. Then Lev and Greg embarked on a friendship that would eventually deliver the violin into Greg's hands, so that one day I would happen to hear it, and set off on the journey that has nonchalantly absorbed four years of my life.

Back in Britain, I had reached Greg's part of the story, how he came by Lev's violin and how he lived alongside it. This landed us straight into such a miserable chapter of his existence that I was surprised he wanted to talk about it at all, but Greg is not shy of admitting that episodes of severe depression used to be a regular feature of his life. Just before encountering Lev's violin for the first time he sank so low that he made two attempts at suicide. 'Heroic failures both of them,' he said, happy to laugh now at the memory. He was working for the Scottish Chamber Orchestra and playing another Italian violin in those days, but with his plans for the future he had no need of it, and that must be why he offered to sell it to a dealer in Manchester. He drove south through pouring rain, with the violin behind him on the back seat. It was past midnight by the time he arrived, but he refused to go inside. Like a parent giving up a baby for adoption, he preferred to hand the violin over, get straight back in the car, and drive home again.

Greg overslept the next morning, and when he woke he realized at once that he would be late for rehearsal, but worse still, he had no violin to play. This was a problem he would have to solve every day for the next six months, six months of relying on friends and colleagues to lend their spare instruments, six months of being obliged to play whatever they could offer. Some of those borrowed violins were decent, others relatively poor, and soon people began to ask questions. What was he to say when they asked, again and again, 'Greg, what are you doing, playing these ridiculous violins in the Scottish Chamber Orchestra?' Or 'Greg, whatever are you thinking of, recording Mendelssohn symphonies on a toy violin?' He knew he needed to buy another violin, but he had sold his last one so badly that he couldn't afford to replace it with anything nearly so good. A musician will always take a violin on trial before buying it, to see if they are compatible, and this was the beginning of a grim phase of trialling modern violins. At one point he had three violins on trial simultaneously, but none of them had voices he could identify with. That was when he rang his old friend Lev and asked for his help in coming to a decision. Lev came over and listened carefully to Greg playing one violin after another, and then, as Greg tells it, he said 'Why are you bothering to buy a violin, Greg? I have a beautiful violin at home that I could lend you.'

And it was by this confused route, full of unhappiness, chance and mishap, that Greg first laid hands on Lev's violin. When he told me how he drove Lev home, how they climbed the stairs to his flat, and how he watched Lev open a cupboard and pull out a violin case, deep emotion crept into his voice. As he drew a bow across the strings for the first time, Greg realized he was hearing his own voice. 'I felt a total connection with its sound,' he told me. 'It spoke back to me with a dark tone at the bottom of the register that I had found in no other violin, and a sadness in its voice that I have become obsessed with. I can feel the same sadness in myself, and I can express it perfectly through this violin. I had always wanted to make a sound I could be part of, and that was it.' And at that moment, after months in a dreary wilderness of depression and poor performance, Greg knew he had been rescued, because 'suddenly I had the sound I wanted to make, a sound that would say all the things I wanted to say'.

Since the night I heard that sound myself for the first time I had allowed the story of Lev's violin to lead me wherever it liked. I had caught trains and planes for it, climbed mountains for it, spent days in libraries and woodyards, attended violin-making school, and even gone to Russia for it. Looking back, I struggled to understand how the voice of a worthless violin could have enlisted me into such dedicated service, and, not for the first time, I began to think of ending our strange relationship. And yet months earlier Florian Leonhard had said something that left me certain its story was unfinished. He told me that dendrochronology reports are the scientific proof that he and other dealers use to back up their conclusions about provenance. Scientific proof? From the moment he said it I had been wondering what a dendrochronology report on Lev's violin might do to the story I had been piecing together for so long. Would a test endorse its Cremona credentials and validate the story I had told? Or would Lev's violin be revealed as an imposter in my life, and Greg's too? The prospect of a test tempted and repelled me in equal measure. Dendrochronology struck me as the antithesis of everything I loved about Lev's violin and its story. It was a perfect expression of our twenty-first-century hyper-vigilance and intolerance of uncertainty, while the story of Lev's violin seemed to belong to an ancient, soft-edged, candlelit place where mystery could still flourish and truth might turn out to be approximate. What to do? Undecided, I realized I had more in common with the people queuing up to kiss the relic of St Anthony's tongue in Padua than I had supposed. If I wanted to discover the absolute truth about the age and origin of Lev's violin, I only had to ask Greg for a photograph of the tree rings on its belly, and send the image off to a dendrochronologist. But like those pilgrims in Padua, I was nursing a story about an object that I desperately wanted to believe, and although there were scientific tests capable of proving or disproving both of our stories, none of us seemed inclined to make use of them. That said, I was very curious about dendrochronology. In the past we had to rely on the instincts and opinions of dealers and connoisseurs when it came to defining the provenance of Old Italians, but now we have a scientific process that can strip away centuries of expert opinion and reveal absolute truths. It was this that interested me when I made an appointment with the dendrochronologist.

All About Rings

A Dendrochronology Test and Its Result

Peter Ratcliff originally trained as a violin-maker and restorer, and the walls of his workshop in a narrow side street in Hove, East Sussex, are lined with instruments waiting for his attention. Wait on, violins, Peter doesn't make or mend you any more because he has taken up a much more dramatic profession. Sometimes the results of one of his tests can bring a violin auction to a halt, and sometimes they can alter the value of an instrument by thousands of pounds, or even hundreds of thousands.

Peter's work is all about growth rings. Children are taught that a tree lays down one ring a year, so they can tell how old it is by counting the pattern of concentric rings in the trunk when it is felled. As a child I used to feel sorry for trees, whose birthdays could only be celebrated after they were dead. Growth rings in a tree grown at low altitude can actually tell us much more about the life of a tree than its age. They are a record written in wood of all the peaks and troughs of its existence, a memory of hot summers and harsh winters, of droughts, floods and changes of light when nearby trees fell or were felled. Trees grown at low altitude are so responsive to the nuances of their environment that spruce trees growing quite close together can have radically different ring patterns. However, the resonance wood used for making violin bellies is always taken from trees felled in high-altitude forests like Paneveggio, where uniformly poor soil and cold winters are the dominant influence on growth, so that all the trees growing in the same area will tend to exhibit very similar ring patterns. Peter's profession depends on this similarity, and he explained that, if I were ever to decide to have Lev's violin tested, he would do it by cross-referencing the yearly variations in the ring growth of the spruce in its belly with the growth patterns of all the other samples in the database where he keeps information drawn from the roughly 5,000 instruments he has tested himself, 150 of them made by Stradivari in Cremona, information shared by other dendrochronologists from all over the world, and the regional reference chronologies helpfully published by the International Tree-Ring Data Bank. The cross-referencing between a photograph of the tree rings in the belly of Lev's violin and all this data would be done by computer software specially developed for him in Ukraine. 'I found a guy on the internet,' he told me, 'and I just sent him a statistical algorithm for cross-dating one series of rings against another. We had been developing the software together for at least three years before I realized that he can only have been about thirteen years old when we started.' Perhaps Peter's software originated as a school IT project in Ukraine, who knows, but today it is the basis for a business so successful that after ten years on the job he is known as one of the leading dendrochronologists in the world.

When the software reveals a very strong correlation between the sample he is testing and a ring pattern on the database, Peter will plot the two patterns on a graph. If they are very similar it suggests a strong relationship between the growth of the two trees, but Peter never jumps to conclusions. 'Sometimes you can analyse an unknown violin that comes up as a same-tree match with a Stradivarius, but you have to use your common sense, and if it doesn't look like a Strad, it probably has nothing to do with him.'

And that's dendrochronology all over, a combination of hard science and common sense, a fixed point in the uncertain world of the violin trade, where so much of a violin's value rests on assumptions about an instrument's age and provenance. I still felt squeamish about commissioning Peter to test Lev's violin, and yet as time passed the temptation to test the story of its origin in Cremona against scientific evidence gathered strength. But how would Greg respond if Peter's report exposed an entirely new history for his violin? I had often seen them perform together by now, and watched the violin settle on his shoulder with the insouciance of a child settling on your hip to be carried. Lev's violin had given Greg the voice to express everything he wanted to say, and although he had always treasured it for that gift, I knew that he also loved it as the unrecognized, bastard child of some great aristocratic Cremona family. That was its image in his mind, and I couldn't begin to guess how he would feel if Peter's report dislodged it. And what about me? What would I feel if it turned out that Lev's violin didn't come from Cremona? Having taken in and then rejected so many things from my mother's house after she died, I had already learned that stories about provenance were what I valued most about the objects in my life. Affection for them had opened my eyes in ways I can only explain by describing a field of long grass I walk through almost every morning. On a cloudy day it is unremarkable, but bright summer mornings reveal a glistening fabric of spiders' webs and strands between the stems of every clump of grass, dock and thistle. For some time now the webs festooned over the field have reminded me of the stories clinging to the objects all around us. It takes a certain fall of light to reveal them, and even then we sometimes choose to ignore what we see, just as I had done with the stories of many of my mother's things. So much of what I lost when she died had been invisible to me that the story of Lev's violin had come to seem strangely precious, and I had no idea how I would feel if it turned out to be untrue.

I don't know who I worried about most, Greg or me, but I did it for weeks on end before eventually deciding to go back to Glasgow and talk to him. We sat in his kitchen, and over the first mug of tea he explained that he and the violin had been through a tough time since we last saw them, for they had both suffered serious injuries. Greg's injury was to a finger, which he had crushed in the faulty door of a recording studio. This made playing impossible for a couple of months. When he recovered and opened the violin's case at last, he found that, not content with its usual trick of coming unstuck at the seams, Lev's violin had used its spare time to make a grand gesture of sympathy. Its neck had come right off, so that it lay in its case looking as helpless as a puppet with broken strings. He took it to a well-known luthier in Edinburgh, an old friend who had often repaired his violin before, but when he came back to collect it this time, Greg got a stern warning. 'The neck may last a week,' his friend said, 'six weeks or six months, I really have no idea. But whatever happens, I will never work on this violin for you again, and so you should really begin to think about replacing it.'

Replacing it? I could hardly believe what I was hearing.

The luthier went on to say that, although he would like to make the replacement himself, the person Greg needed was Melvin Goldsmith, because, as he so modestly put it, 'he is better than me.'

Greg and the violin returned to work, and although he worried about it all the time, the neck seemed to be holding. Until it didn't, and then it was a horrible, torn, blistered thing that Greg tried to take back to his friend. Despite those dire warnings, the luthier must have relented, because they made an appointment for the following week. However, on the day before they were due to meet, Greg's friend died, suddenly, shockingly, at the age of fifty. And as for Lev's violin, he had told Greg he wouldn't work on it again, couldn't work on it again, and now he was gone.

Greg began to do the rounds of other luthiers. It was a much more serious repair this time, and everyone he spoke to quoted such astronomical prices that he began to think of Lev's violin as beyond repair. Unhappy and uncertain, he went to see his friend Martin Swan, a well-known musician and composer turned violin dealer. Martin changed the grim outlook for Lev's violin by saying he could get it repaired at a fraction of the price. This should be the turning point in a sad chapter of the violin's story, but something else must have splintered at the same time as its neck, because instead of accepting his offer, Greg left Lev's violin with Martin and went home to consider his options. Should he spend thousands of pounds on resurrecting it, or should he commission Melvin and start again with a new instrument? Over the years Greg had sometimes felt the violin sing with relief after a repair, but each time it came home it was subtly different. What if he had it repaired now, and found he didn't like the way it sounded any more?

These were Greg's thoughts when I asked if he would mind me sending photographs of Lev's violin to a dendrochronologist for testing. 'Why should I mind?' he replied. It was that simple.

To my mind the story I was following had always been like a parcel wrapped in many layers of paper, and because the music of Lev's violin went on and on, it was always on the move, always circulating like an endless game of pass-the-parcel. But now two things happened almost simultaneously, and the music stopped.

First came Peter's report. Dendrochronology can't prove the provenance of a violin, but it can disprove it, and that's exactly what it did. How could Lev's violin have been made at the beginning of the eighteenth century in Cremona when its belly was made from the wood of two trees felled in the mid-nineteenth century? Italian luthiers sometimes used German wood, but wasn't it strange that both of these trees had grown in the Vogtlandkreis district of Saxony, on the border of Germany and Bohemia (now the Czech Republic)? And when Peter tested the ring patterns against others in his database of German instruments, why did he find so many correlations? Put all this evidence together, and any dendrochronologist would say exactly what Peter said. Lev's violin was much more likely to be a mid-nineteenth-century German instrument than an early eighteenth-century Italian one.

All I had ever wanted to do was explore the story of Lev's violin, and perhaps even prove its Cremona provenance to make a mockery of the dealer who called it worthless. But by having it tested I had destroyed the beautiful myth it carried with it for years, and probably confirmed its zero value as well. After reading the report my first thought was of Greg, but I needn't have worried. He seemed to adjust quite easily to this new identity. 'We bought into a myth,' he said, 'and I like myths. Make-believe is how you live as a musician. There is no real. It's all a metaphor, all implied, all transitory. It's gone as soon as you finish, and you have to make it up all over again.'

After a while I began to wonder why either of us should care whether the story of Lev's violin was true or not. While Greg believed it, everybody around him accepted it too. He played it against

Stradivarius violins and it wasn't shamed; he played it during auditions for top jobs and got them every time. What did truth matter to such a successful team? And anyway, it wasn't long before he found a comforting parallel between the violin's biography and his own. He said he had always felt an outsider in the world of classical musicians, even though everybody accepted his violin because they thought it was an Old Italian. Now, as he put it, 'I'm an outsider playing a violin that's a bit of an imposter,' satisfaction oozing from his voice.

And once I recovered from the shock, I found I really didn't care either. The story had me in its grip for years. Sometimes this felt like a life sentence, sometimes an odyssey, but in the end it had become a habit of mind that subtly changed the way I lived. I have already admitted that I knew next to nothing about violins and their music when I heard Greg play for the first time. Living with the story of Lev's violin for so long has changed all that. When I believed it was a church violin, I filled our house with the joyful sound of all the music I thought it would have played. As time passed, it was as if new synapses formed in my brain, and I began to hear music in a way I had never experienced before. Thanks to Lev's violin I realized that anyone can join the music club, and so I don't feel shut out any more. Something else has changed, too. When I look at the objects living out their lives alongside mine, I realize it is what I believe them to be that matters, not what they really are. And as well as all that, Lev's violin had opened my eyes to a new, violin-shaped version of Italian history.

I had always thought of Lev's violin as eternal, but then Greg explained that it had been feeling its age for some time. It detested damp, sea breezes and air conditioning, and sometimes it would come unstuck at the seams for no apparent reason, often choosing the moment just before a major concert, or even mid-performance, to fall apart. He said that living with it was like looking after an old aunt, whose illnesses and complaints put constant pressure on his working life. And worse still, the people who loved him most had begun to tell him, very gently, very carefully, that although he was still making his own unique sound, it had been steadily dwindling, so that now he was being diminished by Lev's violin. Why had nobody told him this before? They hadn't the heart to mention it, because they all knew he was in love.

All these thoughts were in Greg's mind when he played at the funeral of the violin-maker who had been his friend, and when he met Melvin at the wake afterwards. Their mutual friend had sown the seed of an idea in both of their minds, and Melvin offered to make Greg a new violin without even being asked.

As I listened to Greg talking, I realized the music of Lev's violin had stopped at last, and the story unrolling in front of me for so long had ground to a halt. If I tell you now that the violin is in my office, lying quietly in its case where I can see it whenever I look up from my desk, you will think you know how the story ends. But you don't, because when its music stopped and the last layer of wrapping around the story parcel was torn away, there really was a prize in the middle. It was Martin who found it, when Greg abandoned the violin in his workshop.

He had never believed the story Greg was told about Lev's violin coming from Cremona, and now he had the chance to examine it for himself he recognized it immediately as the product of a small German town called Markneukirchen, which is very close to where the spruce trees for the violin's belly grew. Calling itself 'the Cremona of Germany', Markneukirchen pioneered the production of violins on an almost industrial scale and made itself into one of the richest little communities in Germany. Its violins were exported all over the world, and by the end of the nineteenth century it was doing such roaring trade with America that an American consulate was set up in town. Even more significantly, instruments were also exported in large numbers to pre-revolutionary Russia, which would be a very much more straightforward explanation for the arrival of Lev's violin in Rostov-on-Don than any I had imagined.

Although Peter's report had identified a probable provenance for the violin, it was the expert in Vienna who gave it a proper name. Martin Swan had already spotted its distinctive black-white-black-white-black, five-ply purfling. This was a trademark of the Seidel family, who were one of Markneukirchen's violin-making dynasties. The Viennese expert went further by suggesting it was made by Christian Wilhelm Seidel, who practised from the mid-nineteenth century.

This left a final mystery. Martin Swan knew that Christian Wilhelm had always branded his instruments with the 'Seidel' name, a good, modern system that should have provided Lev's violin with a clear and indelible identity throughout its life. And yet when he searched around inside with an infrared light he could find no trace of Seidel's name. Now he checked the measurements of the arching of the violin's back against the carving marks, and he found it was slightly thinner than it should have been. This indicated that the back had been recarved, and in the process of removing a few millimetres of its thickness, somebody had erased Seidel's name. In part it was this modification that drew me to Lev's violin the first time I heard it, for as well as granting its mysterious anonymity, it gave it the powerful and distinctive voice that seduced me and had always persuaded people to believe the tall story it liked to tell about its provenance.

Light as a bird and lonely now, Lev's violin waits in the corner of my office for its new story to begin. Nothing will happen until someone can afford to mend it, but then it will be free to set off into the world again. Although it will always be old and fragile, this time it will be a named violin with a known provenance and an entirely different place in any value system it might encounter. Until then, it seems to long to be held, to warm itself against my skin. Many of us have some object we love in our lives, but holding this forlorn creature I wonder if objects sometimes love us in return. For Lev's violin feels bereft, as if it were missing Greg, and their busy life together. Sometimes I pore over the scars on its body, each one an undeniable record of some harsh truth about its past. It lies quiet, as unassuming as ever, and as I run my hands over its corners, so smooth they seem wind worn, water worn, it is not wood my fingers gauge, but lack of it.

Coda

There was still one question I found myself asking so often that it has become as irritating and consistent as the flicker of an eyelid after a sleepless night. What if I fell for the sound of Lev's violin because of the Klezmer tune it was playing when I first heard it, and not because of its voice at all? This niggling query went on for so long that in the end I decided to answer my own question once and for all.

You can find a Klezmer band playing somewhere in Italy on any night of the week, and when I went to a Klezmer festival one weekend, I found myself among equal numbers of Jews and non-Jews like me, of men and women, experts and beginners, and even a boy of about ten years old playing the fiddle. In fact there were fiddles everywhere, playing alongside accordions, drums and trumpets, spoons, washboards, cellos, double bass, clarinets, flutes and guitars. I sat down on one of the chairs lining the walls of the hall, but I had forgotten that Klezmer does not tolerate observers. The music wrenched me to my feet almost at once, and then the edge of the undulating circle of dancers opened like a gigantic amoeba to absorb me. Together we danced to music that seemed to trace and re-trace the paths of a familiar conversation, encompassing all the most important things about being human. We considered ancient history and modern life, happiness and suffering, pride and shame, beating out their rhythms with our feet and sometimes our hands, and accepting the good and bad in everything through that insouciant shrug of a tune.

And what about my question? Had I simply fallen under the spell of Klezmer when I heard Lev's violin for the first time, or was there really something about its voice that had been haunting me ever since? People have always talked about the sound of Lev's violin. Lev himself said he had never known a violin like it, it is still the love of Greg's life, and I knew its voice had the power to open my ears to music in a way I had never experienced before. And as for Klezmer, it had been the best possible vehicle for transmitting the sound of the violin to my untutored ear, because it demands no preparation or education by the listener before it cuts to the quick.

So what had induced me to set off on that strange journey in pursuit of a worn-out violin and its story? Was it the Klezmer or the instrument that played it? As the music swept us on around the room, I realized I could never really know.

Acknowledgements

I am especially grateful to Greg Lawson and Lev Atlas, who have been unfailingly generous with their knowledge, company and conversation. My heartfelt thanks also go to Julia Atlas for her kindness to me in Russia.

Among the luthiers I met during my research, I am especially grateful to Melvin Goldsmith, and also to Andrea Ortona, Florian Leonhard, Peter Ratcliff, Stefano Conia and John Langstaffe.

Thank you to La Scuola Internazionale di Liuteria in Cremona for opening its doors to me, and in particular to Angelo Sperzaga for arranging my visit, and to Massimo Ardoli and Alessandro Voltini for welcoming me into their classes. My thanks also to the Consorzio Liutai for their encouragement on my first visit to Cremona. I am also grateful to Andrea Felicetti for introducing me to the trees of Paneveggio.

I would like to thank The Society of Authors for the Authors' Foundation grant that allowed me to complete the travel for this project, and the London Library for its invaluable support through the Carlyle membership scheme.

Many academics and museum curators generously shared their knowledge. Particular thanks go to Professor Stephen Walsh; Professor Eleanor Selfridge-Field at Stanford; Professor Pietro Piussi at l' Univerità degli studi, Florence, and to Colin Harrison, Senior Curator of European Art at the Ashmolean in Oxford.

I am as grateful as ever for the loyal support and unfailing good humour of my agent, Antony Topping at Greene and Heaton, and to all at Penguin, especially my editor, Chloe Currens.

I have depended on the practical help and advice of many friends in Italy. Special thanks, as always, to Valeria Grilli and Jenny Condie, and also to Mariadele Conti, Rossella Pellerino and Julia Bolton

Acknowledgements

Holloway. Thank you to Professor Stephen Hugh Jones for his kindness and enthusiasm, and to Marina Benjamin, Deborah Moggach, Catherine Janson, Emma Beynon and Will Bullough.

Finally, love and thanks go, as ever, to Alex Ramsay, and to Connie Ramsay for always listening, wherever she was in the world.

Index

Index